The Goode Life:

Memoirs of Disability Rights Activist Barb Goode

By Barb Goode
with Jim Reynolds

Spectrum Press

A DIVISION OF SPECTRUM SOCIETY
FOR COMMUNITY LIVING

Spectrum Press, a division of Spectrum Society,
Vancouver, B.C., 2011

Contents

To Mom and Dad –
words cannot express how much
you meant 'two' me.
Lots of love, Barb.
I miss you every day.

Acknowledgements - Thanks

This book could not have been written without the help of many people. My sincerest thanks to:

Harold Barnes, B.C. People First, Merrilyn Cook, Gunnar and Rosemary Dybwad, Al Etmanski, Fred Ford, Jule Hopkins, Aaron Johannes, Chris Lee, John Lord, Kim Lyster, Shelley Nessman, Maureen Olofson, Avril Orloff, Peter Park, Susan Stanfield, Jack Styan, Karla Verschoor, and all the organizations and people I have worked with over the years – you know who you are.

Special thanks to Jim Reynolds for helping me to get my ideas into some kind of order and for making sure my story is told in my words. Special thanks to Chris Lee, too. His early research helped get my book project started. Also, extra thanks go out to Shelley, Susan and Aaron for their assistance with the editing and formatting. Thanks to Spectrum Society, www.101friends.ca and the Spectrum Press for publishing my book.

Thanks to U.N. Secretary Jean Vanier for allowing me to use a poem from his book Tears of Silence.

Thanks to the folks at Inclusion Press (www.inclusion.com), who came up with PATH (Planning Alternative Tomorrows with Hope), the fun planning tool that helped me to fulfill my goal to write the life story you are about to read.

Throughout this book, on each chapter heading, you will see small illustrations taken from the PATH that Avril Orloff was the graphic facilitator for. I will talk more about what the PATH process meant to me later, but I wanted to thank Avril for allowing us to use her beautiful drawings about my life in this way.

If I have forgotten anyone, and I'm sure I have, I apologize. I'll put you in the second edition!

Barb

Introduction: Why did I want to write my story?

I guess the first thing that comes to mind is that writing a book about my experiences in the disability rights movement is something I've been thinking about a lot over the years.

In fact, in a forward I wrote back in 1990 for a plain language booklet called *The Right to Have Enough Money*, I talk about self advocates writing books to help other self advocates:

> *This is the first in a series of books for self-advocates, and others, to help us have a better life through knowing more.*
>
> *Self-advocates need people to help us write books. Topics we'll be covering in our series are issues that are important to everybody's lives. They include poverty, money self-advocates receive from the government, friendship, and other issues that affect our lives.*
>
> *We are getting famous Canadian writers to assist us in writing the books: for example, June Callwood.*
>
> *It is very important for self-advocates and others to have books that we can understand. We hope that self-advocates can use these books to learn new and interesting things.*
>
> *I want to thank those who had faith in us and who assisted us to write these books. It is a great opportunity. This is something that has never been tried this way before, and self-advocates need to be more involved in projects like this.* (forward, to June Callwood, *The Right to Have Enough Money: A Straightforward Guide to the Disability Income System in Canada (Rights, Justice, Power Series).* G Allan Roeher Inst.,1996.

For more than twenty years people have been telling me that it would be neat, an interesting story, if I were to write my autobiography.

Mmm hmm – many people have been encouraging me through the years to write my story.

I guess I have a different way of seeing things than most people. I don't know....

For instance, I have always said, "Don't judge someone before you at least try to see the situation through their eyes."

Yes, I think I see things differently than other people might. I always try to put myself into other peoples' shoes.

I don't like labels, because they encourage pre-judging someone based on their disability, rather than have the focus be on the person's abilities.

We all go through things differently.

My book is partly directed to people who might be living in ways that are not ideal. A lot of people are still living in institutions. A lot of people are put into group home settings without their input, or the input of their family and friends. They are not moved in with friends, or even people they know.

They are most often placed with complete strangers. In the group home I lived in, I didn't know anyone very well. Even after a year and a half, for a number of reasons, I never got to know my housemates all that well.

Many people living in institutions and in group homes have no unpaid friends.

We need to change things so that everyone can have a goode life. People with disabilities want the same things as everyone else in this world, and it's not fair that so many are not able to use their gifts and not living how they want. If my book helps some people to have a better life, I will be very happy.

My book has photos, interviews, poetry, and history – I have even included some of my favourite recipes and quotes , because these things are all important for a goode life.   From an early age, my mother saved recipes for me because she assumed I'd be cooking for myself one day. My parents assumed I would need recipes.   There will be stories about how people with disabilities have been treated over the years (some "goode" and some bad). There will be stories of successes.

I think it is important for people to hear some of the upsetting things that happened to me in my life, so that they can learn from them, and then maybe they can avoid the same things happening to them in the future.

I don't want to sound negative, but I feel it is important for people to understand some of the bad things that other people have gone through in the past, and (in some cases) are still going through today.

I hope that my book encourages people to keep working towards full equal rights for people with disabilities. If people start taking for granted the rights that so many of us worked so hard for, we could easily lose them.

My parents taught me about independence. They always tried to encourage me to do things that other people didn't think I could do.

Yes, my parents taught me to think for myself and to do things for myself, and I will always be grateful to them for that.

Where did my parents get their ideas? I think they just did what they thought was right. They were both very humble and unassuming, and they brought me up to be like them. I don't know how to be any other way. Part of what I've found so hard about writing this book is that I'm uncomfortable talking about myself.

As a person with a disability, I sometimes do not feel like I can be open with my emotions. I fear that I will be labeled a behaviorally challenged person.

I'm sorry, but I feel that people without disabilities are freer to be themselves. I look forward to the day when all people are free to be themselves.

If you find my thoughts a little scattered as you read along, smile, you're having the true Barb Goode experience. After all, one of the working titles we had for this book was *Scattered Goode* not Orderly Goode.

And finally, I ask you to forgive me if my dates are a little off. I do my best to remember, believe me, but memories are as individual as the person they belong to, and a lot of time has passed. A lot of things have happened to me over the last few decades – as you're about to find out....

> "Each day is a new opportunity to correct the mistakes of yesterday and to deal with the challenges that face us today."
>
> Father Jerome Le Doux

Here is a quote about the dignity of risk
that I really love:

Risk

To laugh is to risk appearing the fool.
To weep is to risk appearing sentimental.
To reach out for another is to risk involvement.
To expose feelings is to risk exposing your true self.
To place your ideas, your dreams, before a crowd is to risk their loss.
To love is to risk not being loved in return.
To live is to risk dying.
To hope is to risk despair.
To try is to risk failure.
But risks must be taken, because the greatest hazard in life is to risk nothing. Those who risk nothing, do nothing, have nothing, and are nothing. They may avoid suffering and sorrow, but they cannot learn, feel, change, grow, love, or live. Chained by their attitudes, they are slaves, they have forfeited their freedom. Only a person who risks is free.

Anonymous

Plain Language

My friends jokingly call me the Queen of plain language. I strongly believe that people with disabilities should be able to understand written and spoken language, especially if it is for and / or about us.

Some people think it is just doctors who talk in a way that few people can understand. But it's not. Teachers, the people in government who are supposed to help us, almost everywhere you go. Lawyers, for example, who are supposed to make things clear. My parents passed away recently. Their will was so complicated, but when I asked questions about it, the lawyer explained it in a way which I still could not understand. I feel that if I want to know something about my parents' will, I should be told in a way that I can easily understand.

So, I mean this to be a plain language book. I hope that everyone will understand what I am writing. But if there is anything that you have a hard time understanding, I encourage (suggest to) my readers to ask a friend to explain it to you. Some of the harder words are defined in the glossary at the back of the book. A glossary is a list of words with easy to understand explanations.

I have taken part in many projects putting difficult documents into plain language. A few years ago I was working with a friend on a plain language project. The project leaders had asked us to read a bunch of papers they had written. They wanted us to re-write them into plain language, but none of the leaders were available to help us. We were given only one week to finish.

There were about 15 to 20 different long papers (a big stack). My friend and I decided to split them, and we each took half. My friend had no disability.

Out of this stack there was one example that they had already put into plain language. But when my friend and I compared both versions, the meanings seemed totally different to both of us.

The original papers, meant for people without disabilities, were all very complicated, and we found the job impossible to finish. What eventually happened was my friend and I read about two or three papers each. We were frustrated because the writing was too difficult and there was not enough time.

The project leaders gave us an "A" for effort, but my questions were, "What is the point of putting it into such complicated language in the first place?" and, "Why was the meaning of the plain language example they gave us so different from the original document?"

People with disabilities should be able to understand language that is meant for them, and about them, and the original meaning shouldn't change in the plain language translation.

My plain language approach: I usually do these projects with someone else. In particular, it really helps to have somebody who was involved in the original version. They can explain what I don't understand, or what I don't think everyone will understand, and then help me to think about it in another way; in a way that will be accessible to everybody.

Bus schedules and community centre guides are perfect examples of documents that should be written in plain language. Also, medical forms and government papers should be easy to understand. Plain language is about accessibility for all.

I hope one day that my book will come out as an audio version, and maybe even in Braille. (Great news, at my last proof-reading meeting I discovered that this will be available as an e-book to download!)

Listening
"If you are going to work with me,
you have to listen to me.
And you can't just listen with your ears,
because it will go to your head too fast.
If you listen slow, with your whole body,
some of what I say will enter your heart."

Barb Goode

"On Listening"

When I ask you to listen to me and you start by giving advice, you have not done what I asked.

When I ask you to listen to me and begin to tell me why I shouldn't feel that way, you are trampling on my feelings.

When I ask you to listen to me and you feel you have to do something to solve my problem, you have failed me, strange as it may seem.

Listen! All I ask is that you listen, not talk or do . . . just hear me.

When you do something for me that I can and need to do for myself, you contribute to my fear and inadequacy.

And I can do for myself. I'm not helpless. Maybe discouraged and faltering, but not helpless.

But when you accept as simple fact that I do feel what I feel, no matter how irrational, then I can quit trying to convince you and get about the business of understanding what's behind this irrational feeling. And when that's clear, the answers are obvious and I don't need advice.

Author Unknown

The 1950's and 60's

I was born (as all goode autobiographies should start) at the Royal Jubilee Hospital in Victoria. That was in 1954. By the way, I am proud to tell my age, even though some people get worked up and tell me that women should never tell their ages. Personally, I don't understand why people are ashamed to tell their ages.

We find way too many things to be ashamed of in our lives, when what we should be doing is focusing on our strengths and our achievements.

Lost and Found

My family moved to New Westminster when I was 7 or 8 months old and stayed there until I was about 5 or 6 years old, when we moved to North Vancouver.

Those days in New Westminster, even when I was only around 3 or 4 years old, I was very adventurous, or so I've been told. My Mom used to tell a story from when I was 4 years old and my brother was 2. It was a foggy morning. We were playing out in the yard and I guess I decided to go for a walk on my own – little Miss Independent. Mom came out to the yard and she couldn't find me. She instantly panicked and began looking all over the house and yard for me, but I was not there.

My Mom immediately called the police. The police arrived and they all went out looking for me. They found me playing in a mud puddle 2 houses down, having the time of my life in the fog.

Before age 5, some friends of my parents told them they should to move to Victoria where there were more options for me: doctors and day programs and such. I wasn't talking yet, so these same friends recommended that my parents send me to a special boarding school.

But my parents said no, I was going to stay with them.

I didn't talk until I was 7 or 8 years old, but my Mom said many times that I more than made up for lost time. I'm still making up for it!

Anyway, around this time, we moved to North Vancouver. I went to a kindergarten there for about two years.

When I was 7 years old I went to a regular school – Westview Elementary. It was a weird school. For one thing, Westview had separate boys' and girls' entrances. The entrances were separate, but the classes weren't.

It was mainly a regular school, but they put me into a completely segregated special needs class of only seven students. They never let me try any of the regular classes. The kids in our special needs class hardly ever saw any of the other kids that went to the regular classes there, but some of the regular students would make fun of us when we did see them.

Back then, I don't remember having any friends over. I'm not sure why. Maybe it was because my friends lived farther away, but I often wonder if it was because of the fact that their disabilities made it too much extra work for the other moms.

These days, lots of people call me their sister, but in reality I have just my one brother.

Here, I think, is a goode early example of the double standards I have worked against for my whole life.

My brother is two years younger than me, as I have already mentioned, but we started school the same year – he started at 5, but I wasn't allowed to start until I was 7.

We never got to go to the same school. His school was a bit closer than mine, so he was allowed to walk, while I had to take the bus to school with my Mom. I felt like my family had less trust that I could do things on my own. I felt, just because I wasn't talking perfectly yet, that everyone automatically assumed I couldn't do anything else very well, either – which was just not true.

We had a neighbour kid who went to the same school – Westview Elementary. Our mothers would walk us to the bus stop.

His Mom got him onto the bus and then went back home, the regular bus, not the "bunny bus." But my Mom came all the way to the school with me. That is, until our bus driver, Harry, told my Mom that she didn't need to come along every time. He told my Mom that he would make sure I made it.

Every day he would say to our moms, "Back to bed ladies, they'll be fine with me."

Harry was the person who started me really thinking about my independence; that I could do things for myself that other people didn't think I could. It's strange to think that this was 50 years ago and most people then would not have thought like Harry.

To this day, I remember that Harry would let us warm our hands on the bus heater on cold winter days. One day, Charlie took over the afternoon portion of Harry's route, and he was just as nice.

One time, when I was around 9 or 10 years old, we got out of school early for some reason. I remember it was a hot dog day, and they let us go right after lunch. I was with a close friend of mine with a disability. We were wondering how to get home. His mom usually came to pick him up after school, but that day he would have had to wait hours for her. I usually took the bus, but I had spent all of my bus money on hot dogs. And so I convinced my friend to walk home with me. It was a one and a half mile walk.

I was proud of myself for helping my friend get home safely. It was his first time going anywhere independently, and it was the happiest I had ever seen him.

My friends' mom was very upset though, because she didn't think we should be so independent, or that was my way of looking at it. After that, she didn't like me anymore, because she thought I had put her son at risk. She refused to allow us to be friends, and then she switched him to a school just for kids with disabilities.

School Days

I'd hate to add up all the friendships I've lost like that. It makes me emotional just to think about it.

I got my diagnosis at a doctor's appointment when I was less than 10 years old. The doctor took my parents into another room and told them. But my parents didn't tell me until many years later. I wondered sometimes why they took so long to tell me. I thought it was my right to know. In any case, I knew long before they told me. You don't need to be a genius to figure out how come you are in the special needs classroom.

Today, I realize that my parents didn't want to label me. They wanted me to go through as much of my life as possible without the damage and prejudice that labels cause.

Now I realize that the younger you label a person, the harder it is for them to think of themselves as people first and not disability first.

I didn't like Westview Elementary that much, and so my parents decided to switch me from there to another elementary school much further away.

Westview Elementary School (I'm holding the sign)

From age 11 to 14, I went to Queen Mary Elementary School. It also had separate entrances for boys and girls. Again, I was put into all special needs classes. Again, our class was totally segregated from all the other students. And, if anything, I felt even more picked-on there. I was older, and so I think I was more aware of the teasing.

Because I don't appear to be disabled, people sometimes thought that I was pretending. Even myself, I vaguely remember thinking back then, "Why am I in a special needs class?" "Why can't I do things independently like my brother?"

When I started at Queen Mary, I had a friend with a disability. But they didn't know she had a disability until later, so at that time she was in regular classes. While she was in the regular classes she would sit with me on the ride to and from school, but at school she ignored me.

Not that school was all bad - looking back, a lot of people encouraged me. But there was this one teacher - we didn't get along. Even though she was a special needs teacher, I don't think she was the best at helping people with disabilities. She was not very encouraging.

She taught us to knit. I was a very tense knitter and when I made a mistake she would pull the whole thing apart and make me all over start again from the beginning.

My first project was a baby sweater – which, by the way, was very hard.

A childhood friend of mine who was a boy, and in the same class, had woolly socks on and was resting his feet on the desk. The teacher told him in a very serious voice to take his stinky, dirty feet out of the classroom!

My grades dropped when I was in this teacher's class. My parents weren't very happy about it. I was supposed to stay with the teacher for another year, but thanks to Mom and Dad, I was moved to another classroom.

The new class I went into was much better for me. My new teacher was from Scotland and I liked her a lot. One time, in her class, we had a sale, but with fun activities. It was like a fair, but inside the classroom. There were things for sale and things to do, like a fish-pond where you fished for prizes.

But the main thing I like about our new Scottish teacher was that she was friendlier to us and she treated us the same as everyone else.

Guess which one is me! (middle row, left, beside teacher)

I remember around this time having speech therapy at home with another student. Sometimes it would be at my house and sometimes at hers. I didn't think I needed speech therapy, and I thought the therapist was impatient. I can't remember too many details about it – I think because there were some parts that I don't want to remember.

On a much happier note, it was around this time that I first met my lifelong friend, Jule (Jules) Hopkins. It was 1968 or '69 at Outdoor School in Squamish, where Jule was a counselor. Jule's nick-name was "Smiley."

This photo of Jule and me is one of my favourites – we're both so happy in it!

I asked her recently if her name was Jule or Jules. I have always called her Jule. She told me her real name was Jule and she doesn't know why almost everyone calls her Jules. I had it right all this time!

By the way, Outdoor School was a program that combined outdoor activities with arts and crafts and regular school courses. I loved it!

The 1970's

The Doctor's Appointment

I remember going to the doctor when I was around 16 years old. We came out and Mom said I was fine. Finally, about 20 years later my mother told me that the doctor had said that I couldn't have a child.

When Mom first told me, I was hurt. Of course, I realize now that she was trying to protect me from getting upset, but back when she first told me I worried that she might have been relieved that I couldn't have a baby.

This is hard for me to write, but I think it is important that I put it in the book. You see – I'm sorry – but if I wasn't labeled as handicapped, I would have been told long before. And the way I see it, people with disabilities have a right to know their medical information, and to be told in a way that they can understand.

When I was 16 or 17, and in grade 10, my parents told me that the principal had called them in to tell them that I should stop school and focus on getting a job. This was at Hamilton Junior Secondary. This made my Mom and Dad upset and they said no. They made a deal with the principal that I would stay five more months at Hamilton and then I could switch to Carson Graham High School, where some of my friends were.

I loved Carson Graham. There, I proved myself to a lot of people. I graduated in 1974!

Carson Graham was a regular high school with some special needs classes. I was in a few special classes, but I was also in regular classes for the first time since I started school.

I started volunteering at the Lion's Gate Hospital in North Vancouver while I was still in high school. I worked as a candy striper. The older male patients sometimes called us candy strippers. I liked what I was doing though, because I got to work with all kinds of different people, and I learned a lot.

At the same time, I was volunteering at the old Lion's Gate Hospital as a nurses' aid. When the new Lion's Gate Hospital was built, the old hospital became a nurses' residence. But by the time I started working there, it had been turned into a senior's facility. This job started as a high school work experience course.

Soon it got to the point when that was all I did - I went to school, went to work, came home, ate and slept – and then I would wake up and do it all over again the next day. It wasn't much of a life, from what I remember.

My parents, but especially my Mom, wanted to get me involved in something outside of work. Mom found out about a group of people with disabilities who were meeting regularly to do things together.

I was nervous about the first meeting. I had never belonged to a group before.

Our group started out just meeting to do recreational activities, like softball and games. The biggest thing we did the first year was a trip to visit Penticton.

My Mom saved an article from the North Shore News that talked about how this other group from Portland was setting up an organizing meeting for People First, which would become the largest self-advocacy association run by people with disabilities. In that same article I had explained that becoming a lobby group was the last thing our recreation group originally had on its mind.

I remember being asked whether our recreation group wanted to get involved with the group People First, and I said something like, "Yes, as long as I won't have any responsibilities."

Well, our recreation group went to that People First organizing conference in Oregon. We went with Lynda Palmer and Val Forshaw. Lynda worked for the North Shore Association for the Mentally Handicapped. My friend Shelley Nessman was involved with the recreation group too, but she didn't come with us on this trip.

We all went together in a school bus (Bluebird type) and I remember that at one point long before we even crossed the border, the bus broke down, and either Val or Lynda, I don't remember which one, had to walk to a friend's apartment to phone someone to come and help.

It was a bad start to what ended up being a very goode and worthwhile trip.

Less than a year from then I had become the founding president of the North Vancouver chapter of People First. Go figure.

One time, going down to the United States to another People First gathering with Shelley, a group of us were stopped at the border because we were handicapped and they thought we didn't have anyone with us for support. I remember being questioned by a Customs official about whether there were 'normal' people with us and then wondering whether the 'support staff' had permission to take handicapped people over the border.

It's a big concern of mine that people with disabilities are harassed while traveling – maybe they don't have their papers in order, or they get too nervous to answer questions properly.

I get very nervous when I travel to other countries because of this.

People First

Some people like to argue about which People First group was the first one. To me, it never mattered who was first, what mattered was that groups of people with disabilities were forming to talk about their rights.

At first only about 10 people were really involved with our People First group and maybe 20 more took part in our activities.

When different People First groups would come for conferences in Vancouver, I remember, we would meet out at the Woodlands Institution; a terrifying place.

It wasn't easy being a self advocate in those days. It still isn't, I guess. I remember this one time back then when we were invited to a meeting with people who were not handicapped. It was the first time our People First group had been invited to a meeting like this.

Right away, I noticed that the others like me weren't talking at all, and no one was inviting us to speak up – so I did.

Well, I felt like some of the non-handicapped people, the Normates as I jokingly called them (it was a family joke - my Dad's name was Norm), were upset that I had been so honest and outspoken. They thought it was wrong for me to speak up. I feel it is this attitude of superiority from some people that creates the biggest stumbling blocks to our acceptance in the community.

This is a quote I love:

"Skin is like the paper that a birthday present's wrapped in. There's all different kinds of wrapping paper and it don't matter what the paper is, does it? It's the gift inside that important, isn't it, eh?
Same as us humans. We gotta look inside each other to find the gift. Gotta love each other from the inside out. Shouldn't be too difficult, I reckon."
Anonymous

"It is art that makes life, make interest, makes importance.   And I know of no substitute for the force and the beauty of its process."

Henry James

My North Vancouver Group Home

When I was in my early 20's I wanted to live on my own. But Mom and Dad said no. They wanted me to look for something else (a group home). They were both scared of me being completely on my own, and they thought the group home would be a goode stepping stone towards full independence sometime down the road.

It was just like when people moved from Woodlands and Glendale. They didn't have a choice of who they lived with – I had no choice either.

One of the things I was very uncomfortable with at the group home was the very strict bathing routine. If you didn't follow it exactly, you had to start over from the beginning.

The staff came right into the bathrooms with you to make sure you showered in the "right" order.

The staff at the home also tried to force us to use tampons instead of sanitary napkins, even though they were more difficult for us to use. I had to complain to my parents about it, and then they had to have a talk with the staff. No one that worked at the home listened directly to the residents. It's no wonder, now that I think about it, why it took me so long to feel like an adult. (I'll talk more about this subject later.)

At the group home, I hardly knew my roommates, even after a year. We had different daytime schedules, early bedtimes, long personal care routines, and besides that, we had nothing in common.

There were five staff at the home. Usually two were on at a time and one who worked overnight. When two staff were together, they often talked amongst themselves, and hardly ever included us in any conversations or decision-making.

While I was living at the group home, I still had my job at the Lion's Gate hospital as a nurse's aide, though I wasn't certified yet. There, I helped people with their personal care; I helped them bathe, get dressed, and so on.

Then I would go back to the group home and have the staff coming into the bathroom with me to tell me how to clean myself.

Exactly one year after I moved into the group home, I wanted to move out. But I was told I had to wait six months. During that time I had to practice life skills targets that the staff set for me. I role-played cleaning the house. I was taken grocery shopping, but the staff still did the actual shopping. I did make-believe budgeting which didn't help me at all when I eventually got my own place.

For the last six months or more at the group home they were trying to teach me to do all these things, but I rebelled.

They get you all prepped up, but then you don't really do anything. You have to be able to write up a budget, you have to be able to clean, and you have to pass all these different tests.

What about the average person? Excuse me for saying so, but you don't have to pass any tests to be allowed to move out on your own. You just move. You learn as you go along.

There was no privacy at the group home either. And a lot of group homes are still like that today. As an example, I know a woman who lives with two other women, and she maybe gets 2 or 3 hours alone each day - if she's lucky. Even when she goes to bed, she gets checked on every hour. The staff has to put their initials on an hourly list outside her door to say that they have looked in on her. So when I'm with her now I try to let her be alone.

The Moving Out Story

The night before I moved out of the group home I had packed all of my belongings to get ready. I had to sleep in the spare bedroom, because my room was already being used by a new person.

It was a wet and rainy night, and there was thunder and lightning. It was a strange bed and I was excited and nervous and I couldn't sleep. So I got up to go to the kitchen.

On my way to the kitchen I saw that there was a strange woman sitting in the living room – in my rocking chair. She said she had a gun, and she was making a gun shape with her hand in her sweater pocket. I was scared and I couldn't move.

Finally, the night staff woke up and came to the top of the stairs. She saw the woman and she shoved her outside. I guess the woman had broken in. I watched through the open door as the poor lady stumbled and fell into a ditch.

I was in a daze, but not agitated.

Even though I'd had very little sleep, in the morning when I was supposed to be getting ready to move, I felt unsettled, but strangely calm.

The supervisor came in early that morning to help me with my move. By that time I had been allowed back in my old bedroom, so I could lie down on my old bed. The supervisor was wondering why I wasn't very excited. The night staff told her what had happened, and then she finally understood why I was so quiet.

After this, the night staff read to us from *Anne of Green Gables* and I began to feel more collected.

The move wasn't as smooth as I would have liked it to be, but I was moving along the road to independence, so that's all goode. It certainly didn't help to have a strange woman break into the house the night before my move, but you can't change what has already happened, I always say.

I moved into a bachelor suite in North Vancouver. I was happy, because it was close to my parents. I was doing most things on my own. I still had a little help from the group home staff – mainly to buy groceries.

This one time I was out on my balcony talking with a friend, and a woman walked right into my place without asking – without even knocking. I had only been on my own for a short time. She never even introduced herself, but I found out later that she was a woman from the Ministry. She had been sent to check that I was living at the right place and that I was keeping my place nice.

Another day, a different woman barged in and checked my fridge. She also just marched right into my apartment without knocking. She startled me. And I remember her saying that I didn't eat right. She wasn't telling me, she was talking aloud as she filled out her form. Well, I thought, if they gave us more money for groceries....

What does home mean to me? I guess being able to have my own things and be able to do what I want to do. And not be on someone else's schedule – to have my own schedule.

What was my favorite part about moving out? I think the main thing was my privacy. When you live in a group home with two or more other residents and at least two staff, you really don't get much privacy at all, believe me. Real privacy is something you can count on, and there was no private time that you could absolutely count on there.

I sometimes ask people without disabilities to think about what it would be like for them to have a revolving door of different staff around them all day and all night long.

What was the most challenging thing about moving out on my own? I would say, getting used to paying for everything and making my money last. At the group home everything was paid for and we got a small allowance for coffee and things. We didn't have to learn about money. Even when they were training me to budget, it was all make believe, and because it wasn't real, it didn't make much sense to me.

In an October, 1979 Vancouver Sun article, I talked about my work with People First. I was 25 years old and president of the People First North Shore chapter. In the article I talked about integration, independence and having my own apartment.

> *"Friendship is the golden thread*
> *that ties the hearts of all the world."*
>
> *John Evelyn*

One of our first obstacles to integration for people with disabilities was that most people didn't want disabled people living in their neighbourhoods. The newspapers at the time were full of articles about communities blocking group homes and subsidized apartments in their communities. Even some people who were against placing people in institutions didn't want those same people living anywhere near them.

In North Vancouver, in the late 1970's, there were big arguments in city council about housing for people with disabilities. Some councilors wanted "retarded" people to have to apply for a permit to move to housing in North Vancouver.

The group home that I moved to had been in the paper several times. Some people said that the North Shore Association for the Mentally Retarded, as it was known then, pushed through the group home without discussing it with the neighbours. In fact, nothing could be further from the truth.

The Vancouver Sun THURS., OCT. 25, 1979 ★★★★ B 1
BRITISH COLUMBIA

Retarded insist on right to live their own lives

By ROS OBERLYN

"A gentle protest can now be heard throughout the nation from mentally retarded persons who are tired of being overprotected.

"They have begun to object when other people make decisions for them and speak for them, when, with a little time and patience, they could have decided and spoken for themselves." — U.S. report, 1978

Barbara Goode and her fellow members of People First are among the protesters — the mentally handicapped, who are quietly insisting on their rights.

The self-help group, with chapters across Canada, was so named, says Goode, because "we're people first and handicapped second."

"We're not different. We can love each other, we can get married, we can do things in the community. We don't need to be segregated," she said Wednesday.

The 23-year-old woman, president of the North Shore chapter of People First, is attending a national conference on mental retardation this week in Vancouver.

The conference of parents, volunteers, professionals and the handicapped, expected to draw 800 people, is the first chance People First organizers across the country have had to meet.

The mentally handicapped are tired of having others speak for them. And that is a lesson well-meaning volunteers and professionals are still learning.

Take, for example, the information brochure on People First, prepared for the conference.

The Canadian Association for the Mentally Retarded designed the brochure and presented the self-help group with a finished product about themselves.

People First then gave the association their own draft of a brochure. It was their design that was printed and distributed.

In it, the group outlines its goals: To teach people how to talk for themselves, to organize other self-help chapters, to make the public aware of their ability to be part of the community and "to be as independent as possible and to make our own decisions."

Goode has proved it can be done.

From a group home for mentally handicapped women, she moved to her own apartment — a move her parents and

BARBARA GOODE
... "we're people first"

others never thought her capable of making.

Goode has lived in her apartment one year, three weeks and three days. She keeps track of it to the day because, she said, "I'm very proud of that."

At a recent meeting with the North Vancouver school board, People First argued that slow learners should be integrated into the school system.

The group does its work through meetings and social events. Money to carry out its projects is raised through membership dues and car washes, dances and bottle drives.

"Our dream is to spread the news about People First across Canada," the brochure states. "Through our movement we will gain support and training to become more independent.

"It may take us a long time, but we'll get there in the end."

The North Shore Association had invited all the neighbours to a meeting with staff and board members, but no one showed up. They mailed out letters about the home, but no one responded.

People didn't understand the issue. Some of them thought the group home would be filled with criminals who would bring down the value of their homes.

But even after the disabled residents moved in (all nice, quiet girls), a doctor's wife started a petition to get them out. The petition stated that the North Shore Association had broken by-laws by

WITH PRESSURE ON DISTRICT COUNCIL

Residents block home for

retarded

forcing their way into an area of single family dwellings, and that having undesirables living nearby would affect the value of their homes. Sixteen close neighbours signed it.

By 1978, the North Vancouver city council had changed the by-laws so that 60% of the neighbours living within 200 feet of a proposed group home had to consent to it. One home was bought by the North Shore Association, but in the end only 50% of the neighbours gave their consent, so the group home couldn't open. The owner of the house then sued the Association for failing to complete the sale of the house.

Letters to the Editor

GROUP HOME on Edgemont...neighbors never responded.

Neighbors did not respond

July 25/79

GROUP HOMES GET A BREAK

North Vancouver City Council Monday decided it should take a more lenient attitude towards permitting "group homes" in the City for people of special needs.

home would h favor of the before Counc mit it to be Such homes permitted metres of e:

But by this time the Ministry of Human Resources was committed to closing all the institutions, so all those people had to go somewhere. The Provincial government started to put more pressure on the municipalities to allow disabled people to move in.

In 1979, the North Vancouver city council announced that they had decided to be more lenient in allowing group homes to open. But in the end all they did was create a long list of rules and regulations for community living agencies to follow. Neighbours in many areas still had the power to stop homes from opening near them.

Some people in support of community living were still being booed by other residents attending council meetings.

In a way, all this media attention was goode. It started an ongoing debate about the rights of people with disabilities to be included in "normal" society. Many people changed their minds during this period and ended up coming out in support of people with disabilities living in the community.

In one letter to the editor, from a couple with an adult child with a disability, they wrote, "We close by asking: if not here, then where will the children be accepted? Please let us know. We'll gladly ask the Association to move the project there." It was the late 1970's and their only other choice for her, besides staying at home with them, was an institution.

What has happened to our society that we let a few unfeeling bigoted people spoil a fine project that is long overdue.

"letter to the editor"
from a group home supporter

More and more people writing in to the editorial pages of the newspapers supported community living. My Mom saved an entire scrapbook of letters to the editor about this subject. The later ones were a lot more in favour of closing institutions and welcoming people with disabilities into their communities.

Barb's Hawaiian-style Turkey Casserole

6 oz noodles

2 Tablespoon butter

2 Tablespoon chopped green pepper

1 Tablespoon all purpose flour

1 cup milk

1 can (10 oz) condensed cream of mushroom soup

2 cups chopped turkey

1 can (19 oz) pineapple chunks drained

1 Tablespoon chopped pimento

1 Tablespoon Worcestershire sauce

Salt and pepper to taste

1 cup blanched almond halves

Cook the noodles according to the package directions and set aside. In a saucepan, sauté the green pepper in melted butter. Stir in flour. Add milk slowly. Cook until thickened. Add all remaining ingredients plus half the almonds. Layer the noodles and the creamed mixture in a greased two quart casserole dish. Sprinkle the remaining almonds on top. Bake at 350°F for 20 minutes. Serves 6.

The 1980's

In the early 1980's, I attended a national Canadian Association for Community Living (then known as the Canadian Association for the Mentally Retarded) conference at the Bayshore Hotel in Vancouver. My friend, Jo Dickey, helped to organize it. At the conference, I was invited to join the CACL.

With the Canadian Association for Community Living (CACL), I became part of the Consumer Advisory Committee. This committee became part of the legal team that took the "Eve" case all the way to the Canadian Supreme Court. I will talk more about the "Eve" case later, but for now let me explain that the "Eve" case was about the right for people with disabilities not to be sterilized without their consent.

The "Eve" case was the main focus for me all through the early to mid 1980's. Harold Barnes, Peter Park and others were all involved in that case with me.

But I was still working with the Lower Mainland Community Based Services Society (LMCBSS) too. I was the President of the Board for a number of years. We were actively campaigning to close down all the institutions.

The LMCBSS set up group homes (7 or so just in Burnaby alone) for people coming out of the institutions.

We helped people make the move out of the institutions, too. For example, one time I went and accompanied a man from the Glendale Institution in Victoria to his community home in the Lower Mainland. I think people felt safer moving into the community when they had people like themselves right there to support them, *and* if the home and the community were ready for them in advance.

I wanted the institutions closed, but I worried about people coming out and not having a doctor or dentist already set up for them. As it turned out, not all doctors would accept patients with disabilities. I worried about people having to share their homes with strangers, like I did. I worried that there was so often no job training or suitable jobs for people coming from the institutions.

I noticed that all the anxious people from the institutions always seemed to be housed together in the community, and I'm sorry, that just never made any sense to me.

We (the LMCBSS) did the best we could to ease the transition for people moving into the community, and for many years, we also helped to support people in their day programs.

Rights Now

From 1985 to 1989 I worked with Kim Lyster and others on a project with the British Columbia Association for Community Living (BCACL). The project was called Rights Now.

At the beginning of this project, the BCACL was called British Columbians for Mentally Handicapped People (BCMHP). This name was one of the first things we self advocates in the group wanted changed, because we felt that we had to address the negative labels being used to describe us before we could ever expect the community to start to respect us. We are people first.

The goal of Rights Now was to help people with disabilities to overcome the barriers that separated us from becoming a true part of the community. There were three B.C. communities involved in the project.

One of the things we focused on a lot was friendship. People had so many professionals involved in their lives, but many people with disabilities had no friends. This is still true today, sadly.

We also focused on rights for people with disabilities to full equality, and the right to make our own decisions in life. We became aware pretty fast that the systems of staff and paid professionals in our lives actually prevented us from becoming independent. The staff felt (and some still feel) that it was their job to do *everything* for us. My friend, Susan Stanfield, talks about this phenomenon called "learned helplessness." People with disabilities were unintentionally taught to be helpless and dependent.

As I said, the Rights Now project took place in three communities in British Columbia. We went around the Province trying to convince people with disabilities that they could be more independent in their lives, but it was hard. There were so many stumbling blocks.

My personal goal was to be a positive role model to other people with disabilities who wanted to become self advocates.

But in the end, the truth was that many people in the Province, especially people who lived outside of the three communities that were involved in the project, still had no idea about self advocacy, or their rights, or even friendship.

A detailed project report titled "Changing Minds, Opening Doors" was written by Kim Lyster and some of us self advocates after the Rights Now project finished.

"A Final Note", from the Rights Now project paper by John Lord

This project has identified all the ingredients for success in empowering individuals and communities. The Rights Now project began with a huge agenda and met many of its goals. Creating a context for people who have been labeled to begin to express themselves and listen to possibilities and of visions of their own and others made enormous sense.

As the project discovered, however, such a context was not enough. Labeled people also needed the opportunity to meet with regular community citizens around a variety of issues and interests. As relationships began to form between handicapped and non-handicapped people, we saw community organizations such as churches and community groups begin to extend their blanket of welcome and become true community associations.

Finally, it is worth reflecting on who the real leaders were in the Rights Now project. While staff played vital roles as enablers, it was labeled people themselves who shared the vision and sparked the enthusiasm for others to begin the journey towards full citizenship.

Rights Now is some ways represents a first step in a new

form of community work. This community work recognizes that oppressed people themselves must be central to the agenda for change. It also recognizes that the community is the rightful place for people who have traditionally been excluded and labeled. Finally, it recognizes that handi-capped people and non-handicapped people must work in concert to remove barriers and create a sense of community that will be inclusive and tolerant.

At a 1980's award presentation for the
'Woman of Distinction' with
British Columbia Premier Gordon Campbell.

In 1987, I won the Canada Volunteer Award. It is an award that I am very proud of, and I mention it here because my father also won this award, in 1993.

At the 1989 Annual General Meeting of the Canadian Association for Community Living I was granted an Honorary Lifetime Membership. I could not have achieved the things I have over the years without the support of the people I worked with at the CACL, so this honorary membership means a lot to me too. The CACL Lifetime Membership presentation was held in Charlottetown, Prince Edward Island in October 1989.

1989 was the same year that the CACL increased the number of self-advocate directors from two up to six. We also made a commitment to meet with leaders from People First to discuss ways that the CACL could support this important movement.

Here is a short article my Mom saved for me about this presentation:

"Barbara Goode is one of Canada's outstanding self advocates. She was the first self advocate on the CACL board and Executive Committee and the first chairperson of the Consumer Advisory Committee. As spokesperson for self advocates, she helped influence policy regarding sterilization, deinstitutionalization and the (organization's) name change. She is gaining international recognition for her ability to help associations fully involve self advocates in their activities."

I was also still helping to run the Lower Mainland Community Based Services Association.

When I think about it, I guess I have had many different leadership roles working on the self-advocacy movement over the years, but to me some of the most important moments in my life have been about the more personal things, like seeing a friend develop the skills to make her own decisions and choices; helping people to grow bit by bit and be able to do what they want, to learn the skills that I've learned, and to be able to be the best they can be.

It is rewarding to me to see people grow – to see someone who has never talked learn, over 6 months or 6 years, how to speak up for themselves.

The "Eve" Case

In the early 1980's we at People First were all standing up for "Eve"s' right not to be sterilized against her will – or anyone's right. We were against anything happening to a person's body without their consent.

We formed the "Eve" Committee and took her mother to court.

People needed to learn what informed consent means. This goes for any operation, not just sterilization. People with disabilities need to be able to get all the information we need to be able to give our consent. We need to understand all the benefits and all the risks involved. Partly, this is about people without disabilities learning to communicate with people who have a disability in a way that they can understand.

A few of us joined the Consumer Advisory Committee and worked with the legal team on "Eve"s' case. I was the only woman on the Consumer Advisory Committee for a while. Which was strange to me, because I used to think sterilization was only a women's issue.

But my eyes were opened during the case. I found out that it also affected men. I learned this from a goode friend of mine who was on the committee. He said that many men with disabilities had been sterilized without their consent as well.

Legal Crusade of the Eternal Children

"The sterilization of adolescents, often described to them as an appendix operation, is now the radicalizing agent for militants among the mentally handicapped. In sex education classes, group homes and sheltered workshops, they're forming pressure groups and staking a place for themselves inside society – according to the Ontario Association for the Mentally Retarded, 90 percent of the retarded now live in the community....

"...In Ontario, a moratorium has prevented contraceptive surgery on minors since a sturdy showed that 308 children under 18 had been sterilized two years earlier – all but 50 being girls...

"...Now the Supreme Court must address the issue. Sometime in the New Year the court will decide whether 'Eve', a 26 year old PEI woman, will have the tubal litigation her mother requests..."

Maclean's magazine - November 30, 1981

I get emotional reading over this article, partly because I know that people are still being sterilized without their consent. Of course, I get upset about the labels used in these older articles, too.

Another thing, I don't see myself as militant – I just believe in informed consent and equal rights for everyone. I also believe that if people with disabilities don't stand up for their own rights, no one will.

Peter Park and I working on the 'Eve' case

Sterilization was used in some of the institutions as a way to deal with menstruation. Some women were given a drug (depo-provera) which was later found to cause breast cancer.

In the early 80's, most parents still thought that they should have the right to decide about sterilization for their kids with dis-abilities. Most doctors agreed with this.

Even my own Mom, who said she didn't believe in sterilizing me, thought that the decision should be left up to the parents. It shows that parents and family members need to be taught about disability rights too, preferably by the people with disabilities themselves.

"Eve"s' mom saw "Eve" holding hands with her long-term boyfriend and decided right then and there that she wanted her sterilized. "Eve" was already on birth control (also, I believe, without her consent or knowledge), so there was no way she would get pregnant.

I was the same age as "Eve", and I realized that the same thing could easily have happened to me.

In a statement for that same Maclean's article from 1981, I said, "Half the mentally handicapped don't know anything about sterilization." To make it perfectly clear, what I meant by that comment is that people with disabilities were never taught about sterilization, so of course they couldn't make an informed decision.

I think sterilization without consent was just another case of people with disabilities being singled out. Like that Maclean's article goes on to say: *"Why not sterilize alcoholics or child abusers?"*

Further on into the article, they explain more clearly than I could why "Eve"s' original verdict had been appealed.

> *"...In the 'Eve' case, a seemingly clear-cut case of (Eve's) incompetence grew murky when an appeal judge scrutinized the transcript of the trial and doubted the trial judge's opinion. 'Eve's' doctor described her as mildly retarded but virtually unable to express herself. Troubled by the gap between what she could understand and what she could articulate, the appeal judge asked whether she was not capable of informed consent."*

The appeal judge overturned the decision of the original judge, and then the case went to the Supreme Court.

"Eve" was not in court when the decision was handed down. She was hardly ever there. In fact, all through the three trials (the "Eve" case went on and on and on) I had never officially met her.

All the way through the three trials (which took more than 5 years) the lawyers kept saying that "Eve" couldn't talk and could only make the smallest decisions.

Then in the fall of 1989 I met her. I explained to her how important her case was to people with disabilities. Then I was so surprised! I had believed everything that was said about her in court, but the truth was she could talk. She could walk.

I had all these ideas about her; that she needed to rely on other people for everything. No way! There were some things she couldn't do on her own, but I don't accept that people were saying that she couldn't walk or talk or decide whether to have a baby, when it simply wasn't the truth.

At the time, a lot of people told me that I was a mover and a shaker for getting so involved in "Eve"'s case, but I don't necessarily agree. At the time, I just felt really happy to be included on the Consumer Advisory Committee as an important member of the legal team; and of course, I was very happy about the final outcome.

When I think back on it, on the one hand, we won, and I was part of the team, on the other hand I remember an interviewer who stopped Harold and I to ask us questions and when we didn't answer quickly enough, he looked at the person supporting us and got them to answer. I also remember that for the "Eve" case I was traveling to Ottawa one time in a wheelchair because I had hurt my leg. My boyfriend Harold Barnes was with me, and he was also in a wheelchair. Instead of the regular elevator, they put Harold and me in a freight elevator with no sides. It was scary and we felt humiliated. There was no reason what-soever that we couldn't have taken the regular elevator.

Harold Barnes and I

I re-read an interview I did that my Mom saved from the Kinesis newspaper from late 1989. In the interview I said, *"Some people believe that all handicapped women should be sterilized. But why should we be sterilized? Some people say we are not responsible enough to look after our own bodies or that we could never look after kids. I say why sterilize people just because of their labels. In fact, why sterilize anyone?"*

The interviewer asked me how I deal with my anger over the injustices that people with disabilities have had to live with. And I told her, "Sometimes I get angry. I get frustrated. But my big fear – for myself and my friends – is that at any time, if we get angry or upset on the street, we might get thrown into an institution. People tell me I'm crazy – but that's one of my biggest fears in life."

And that's *me* - I'm lucky – I never had to live in an institution. But lots of my friends did, and for them it was awful. I can't imagine how frightened a person who used to live in an institution must feel about the idea of being put back.

The Twentieth Anniversary of the "Eve" Case

2006 was the 20th Anniversary of the "Eve" case. I wrote an article for the Burnaby Association for Community Inclusion (BACI) Newsletter. We had a regular column called Self Advocates' Corner. Here is the article:

> *"Eve" is a self advocate who lived in Prince Edward Island in the 1980's. Her mother saw her holding hands with a man and worried that she might get pregnant. She wanted to get "Eve" sterilized so she could not have kids. October 23rd, 2006 was the 20th Anniversary of the "Eve" Case.*
>
> *At that time I was chairperson of the Consumer Advisory Committee with the Canadian Association for the Mentally Retarded (CAMR), now called the*

Canadian Association for Community Living (CACL). It was a self advocate committee with members from different parts of Canada.

We heard about the "Eve" case and got help to take it to the Supreme Court of Canada. In 1986, the court agreed with us that no one should be sterilized without their consent. (If there is a medical problem, that is different.) In October, 2006, (disability rights lawyer) Dulcie McCallum and I gave a presentation on the "Eve" Case. It brought back a lot of memories for both of us. It was like it just happened.

In the last few years, I have been asked a lot to talk about the "Eve" case. I hope it is not happening as much now – people being sterilized without their consent. It still worries me. It is such a terrible problem. But recently, a woman from Alberta was sterilized without her consent. She lived in an institution at the time. The woman did not find out she was sterilized until she moved out of the institution and she wanted to get married and have kids.

I think people often aren't given enough information to make their own decisions on whether to have children or not. We need to talk more about health, safe sex, and understanding. We need information and workshops (explained in plain language and with pictures) that help us understand as much as we can.

I think it's also very important that we ask questions of doctors, family and friends to help us make the right decision.

After the case was won, a friend of mine without a disability told me this story: "My wife and I didn't want to have any more kids. The "Eve" case made me realize that it was less painful and a simpler operation for me to have a vasectomy, instead of my wife having a major operation."

With Dad

Norm's Turkey Burgers
(My Dad's Favourite)

One third pound ground turkey

One quarter cup chopped parsley

6 medium sized mushrooms chopped

1 Tablespoon breadcrumbs

Add basil, oregano, salt, or pepper if you like.

Mix well. Form into 2 patties. Broil for 8 minutes, then turn and broil for another 8 minutes.

Serve on hamburger buns. You can top your burger with cheese, tomato slices and lettuce.

Use whole wheat or sesame seed buns for a nice change.

The United Nations

In 1982, Nairobi was the host of the Thirteenth Annual Congress of the International League for Persons with a Mental Handicap. I was one of 300 delegates at the Congress, which focused on the rights of individuals with disabilities to respect, relevance, and meaningful opportunities in the community.

I was sponsored by the British Columbia Association for the Mentally Retarded.

Of course, back then everyone was still using terminology which I have disliked since day one – terms like mentally retarded and mentally handicapped. And the order was always disability first, and people second. By this time I had long since adopted the term "community living people."

Anyway, it was my first international conference and I wound up traveling on my own. I was nervous when I received the itinerary, which was twenty pages long, but I tried not to let on to my parents.

As it was, my Mom was very worried about me traveling – just in general. She definitely didn't think it was right for me to be traveling by myself, but I'll give her credit – she tried not to show it either, most of the time. Still, I could always tell when Mom was upset.

Dad was worried too. He thought it would be goode for me to go, but wanted me to travel with someone. Well, there was no one for me to go with, so I had no choice. I went by myself.

The flights were long. I left Vancouver at 6:30 p.m. on a Thursday and was supposed to arrive at Nairobi airport, after a nine hour layover in London, at 8 a.m. on Saturday. But during the trip I was stuck waiting at Heathrow for eight extra hours. I wasn't entirely sure what I should be doing, or where I should be waiting. I'll be honest, at that point I was scared, but I managed. This part of the trip I never told my Mom about. It would only have upset her, and I wanted her to be proud of me. I was proud of myself in the end, because I handled it all independently.

When we landed in Nairobi, I should have felt tired, but I didn't. I guess I must have looked tired though, because everybody kept telling me that I should go and lie down.

Finally I did go and lie down, and I zonked right out. The next thing I knew, a few hours had passed by. I splashed some water on my face and I went out for a walk, feeling even more tired – if that is possible.

All the street signs were different, and the lights too. I was about to cross the street when someone stopped me. I was about to walk directly into traffic! I guess I was still very tired after all. I had maybe a three hour nap, but I hadn't slept for over 36 hours!

JAMBO – that is how they say hello in Kenya. *KARIBUNI* - is their word for welcome, but they told us that it means more than welcome – there is no word quite like it in English.

The various sessions I took part in talked about the roles of organizations, families, self advocates and the people with disabilities themselves in defining and establishing those rights.

The conference included some joint workshops as well as parallel sessions for people with disabilities. To be honest, I had mixed feelings about these parallel sessions. I often felt separated from the rest of the conference when I was in the parallel sessions. Since the main theme of the conference was "partnership," I thought that all the sessions would be for people with disabilities and people without disabilities.

Yes, I have to say, it bothered me that at a world conference on rights and equality for people with handicaps that all the sessions weren't all open to everyone.

Still, it was a great opportunity to get an overview of the issues facing people with disabilities around the world. It was very interesting how much difference there was in the services available in all the different countries, and with all the different cultural values.

Canada may still have a long way to go, I remember thinking, but some countries are way behind us in rights and equality. This is still true today: we still have a long way to go; and many countries have made very little progress at all.

If people only get a few messages from my book, I hope that one of them is that people with disabilities need to keep working for their rights. We need more self advocates to spread the

word, otherwise, I fear, we could lose the rights that we have gained over the last several decades.

As all the conferences I have ever taken part in do, this

Goode gains world view

Barb Goode, long-time self-advocate from Vancouver's North Shore, recently returned from the Thirteenth Annual World congress of the International League of Societies for Persons with a Mental Handicap, held in Nairobi, Kenya.

Goode was one of more than 300 people at the Congress, which focused on the rights of handicapped individuals to respect, relevance, and meaningful opportunities in the community. The various sessions explored the roles of organizations, families, advocates and handicapped persons themselves in defining and establishing those rights.

The conference included joint workshops for all the participants as well as parallel sessions for people living with a handicap. Goode had mixed reactions to this arrangement, noting that she frequently felt separated from the rest of the conference when in the parallel sessions.

Nevertheless, the opportunity to gain an overview of the status of mentally handicapped people world-wide was invaluable, she felt. The quality of services available varied markedly from country to country, she found, based on the cultural values of individual societies.

BARB GOODE

As most conferences do, this international gathering made plain the great amount of work that needs to be done. According to Goode; "The handicapped can't expect somebody to look after all our problems. If we don't work harder at speaking out, other people will make up our minds for us."

Goode's trip was jointly sponsored by CAMR and BCAMR.

Taken from the "Handpress" Newsletter of the North Shore Association for the Mentally Handicapped.

A 1982 article about the Nairobi World Congress

U.N. conference made us all realize how much work we still had ahead of us – that we still have ahead of us today. I keep telling everyone, "You can't forget the past."

Before the conference got started we went on a trip to Nyeri where we were taken on a safari through the Aberdare forest to see wild game animals. We stayed overnight in a nice hotel and got back in time for the conference the next day.

At the end of the conference we went to the Masai Mara game reserve where we saw lions, elephants, giraffes, rhinoceros, leopards, and buffalos, along with many other animals. We stayed overnight in the Safari Lodge and then went back to Nairobi the next morning. It was a full trip!

In 1992, I became the first person with a disability to address the United Nations General Assembly.

> '1992 marked the end of the UN Decade of Disabled Persons. In the decade from 1983 to 1992 the United Nations goal was to put into place the philosophy and goals from the 1981 World Program of Action Concerning Disabled Persons. The goals were: prevention of disability; rehabilitation; full participation and equality for disabled persons in all areas' of life.'

This above paragraph was taken directly from the United Nations newsletter from the conference I attended. I cringe a little when I read over the newsletter today, with all its use of the term "Mentally Handicapped". For instance, in the International League of Societies for Persons with a Mental Handicap (ILSMH) address to the U.N. General Assembly they said, *"Some of you may say 'We do not have enough for our normal citizens, so we cannot consider helping the mentally handicapped people now....'"*

Later in the same address, they said, *"We (the ILSMH) are more than willing to make our expertise available to you. We know how to train the mentally handicapped and their families."*

We were moving in the right direction, but we still had a long way to go!!

I had my speech all ready to go, but the day before the conference a United Nations staff-person asked me if he could have a look at it. He didn't give it back to me until just before I was supposed to go on, and he had changed the tone of my speech quite a bit. He put in words that I would never have said.

Here is the speech as it was re-written:

> *"Ladies and Gentlemen, I am very glad to be here.*
>
> *I speak on behalf of People with mental handicaps.*
> *We are people first – and only secondly do we have a handicap.*
>
> *We want to push our rights forward, and we want to let other people know that we are here.*
>
> *We want to explain to our fellow human beings that we can live and work in our communities.*
>
> *We want to show that we have rights and responsibilities.*
>
> *Our voice may be a new one to many of you, but you better get used to hearing it.*
>
> *Many of us still need to learn to speak up.*

Many of you still have to learn how to listen to us and how to understand us.

We need people to have faith in us.

You need to understand that we, like you, do not want to live in institutions. We want to live and work in our communities.

We count on your support to people with a mental handicap and their families. We count on your support to ILSMH and its member associations.

In front of the world flags outside the United Nations headquarters in NYC with Victor Wahlstrom (then president of the ILSMH).

Above all, we demand that you give us the right to make choices and decisions regarding our own lives.

We are tired of people telling us to do what they want. Instead, let us all work together as a team!

We all have to find a way of assisting my friends who are unable to speak.

Thank you for having me come and for listening to me."

I didn't feel comfortable saying, "Our voice may be a new one to many of you, but you better get used to hearing it."

And I would never have said "... we demand that you give us the right to make choices and decisions regarding our own lives."

Don't get me wrong, I was proud to be involved and to be the first person with a disability to speak at a United Nations conference; I just wish that I had been included in making the changes to my own speech.

The conference itself focused on the care of persons with a mental handicap in Asia and Africa; some were third world countries and some were not. In many of these places, people were institutionalized in very large institutions, and their staff had no training and no experience.

What is very sad to me, and is something that most people don't know, is that in a lot of these countries this type of care was their effort to copy our western methods of dealing with "defective" people; our method of taking people away from their families and warehousing them and dealing with them in a professional way.

For this conference, the ILSMH put out an excellent book-let called *Training of Persons who Care for Persons with Mental Handicaps*. What they had done was this: two doctors had gone around and trained thousands of staff from these areas of the world. They put a lot of emphasis on including family and friends, which is goode.

They also put a lot of emphasis on the labels that were being used, which were often insulting – labels like diseased, possessed and crazy. Although – *I'm sorry* – but all the way through their training manual the two doctors keep using the term "people who happen to be slow", which I also disliked.

The training they did was very positive though. It was to help staff see their "patients" as people – with exactly the same needs and feelings as them – human in every way.

I can barely bring myself to say this, but some cultures still believe that developmental disabilities are a *deserved* punishment for the sins of the parents. In many cultures, people still do not get a healthy level of care and their lives are shortened because of these kinds of ideas.

It was at the end of this conference that I became the first self advocate on the board of the International League of Societies for Persons with a Mental Handicap (ILSMH). I was the only self advocate on the board until the next conference – then there were two of us.

Here is a sad poem by Jean Vanier from his book Tears of Silence. This poem was also included in the ILSMH Staff Training booklet I just mentioned.

He who is
  Or has been
      Deeply hurt
  Has a RIGHT
      To be sure
          He is LOVED.
Love,
  Not just some passing moment
  A glance however open
  But some deeper compassion
  Radiating permanency.
    Not some morbid curiosity
      Some gushing pity
      Incompetent naiveté
          The cry of burnt-out eyes
                  Wounded bodies
                  Addicted minds
                  Cravings

Can only be answered by some love
In which is felt a strange presence of the eternal
A hope
A new security…

The 1990's

Partnerships in Plain Language

The plain language book called *The Right to Have Enough*  *Money* came out in 1990. It was part of a series of plain language educational books I worked on which included *The Right to Read and Write,* and *The Right to Control What Happens to Your Body,* and several others.

Barb with June Callwood

I was very proud to have worked closely on *The Right to Have Enough Money* with Canadian author, June Callwood.

June Callwood was a famous journalist and writer, and social justice was very important to her. She was made a Companion of the Order of Canada in 2000 – that is the one of the highest honours in Canada. She passed away in 2007.

I was the Assistant Project Coordinator for this educational series. Our team of self advocates and advisors came up with tons of helpful ideas and suggestions for this book and for the others in the series.

For this project we wanted a plain language guide about the Disability Income System in Canada, and we wanted it to be fun and educational at the same time. So, as well as easy-to-understand articles, we also used checklists,

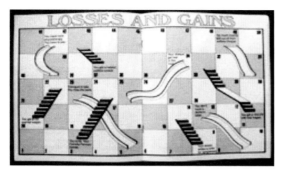

This is a game we called Losses and Gains, which was included in the guide The Right to Have Money.

graphs, drawings, question-and-answer comics, a dictionary, and even a couple of games.

By 1990 I had become involved with other self advocacy groups. Some people will not agree with what I am about to say, but some will. I think there is room for all kinds of different groups of self advocates, and that different groups represent and include different kinds of self advocates. Some see this as a time of splitting apart in our history, but I see it as a time when more people stood up to be counted, in different ways. I wanted to be part of that, and I didn't want to argue. As an aside, it boggles my mind that people spend so much time talking about money, or arguing about politics, rather than just getting things done.

As self advocates, we would work together with advisors on issues of self advocacy. We at the B.C.A.C.L. put out a quarterly newsletter called *The Voice*. In it we answered questions and wrote articles about housing, programs, and services available to self advocates.

I was still involved with People First, too, as well as the Lower Mainland Community Based Services Society.

People First also put out a magazine back then. It was called *The National Organizer*, and it was sent out all across Canada.

By the early 1990's, there were a number of Provincial People First organizations, and our priority was to form a National People First group – People First of Canada.

Around this time I was interviewed by self advocate leader Peter Park on the topic of "Why a National People First is Needed" for the February issue of the *National Organizer*. Here is the interview:

Peter: When did you hear about People First?

Barb: I heard about it over a cup of coffee in someone's kitchen, but at the time the name People First did not exist.

Peter: When did People First begin in British Columbia?

Barb: People First began as the name of a conference in Salem, Oregon in about 1977, where I went with some other people from British Columbia. We brought the name People First back to our local group in Burnaby, British Columbia in the fall of 1977.

Peter: Why is People First Important?

Barb: It gives members a chance to speak up for themselves, and the members help each other by telling their personal stories.

Peter: Where are you now?

Barb: We want to have more and stronger local and Provincial groups. We want to form a National group.

Peter: I know this is a loaded question Barb, and you don't have to answer if you feel uncomfortable. Where do you see People First going in the future; e.g. the year 2001?

Barb: I see a member in British Columbia (with communication challenges) able to talk to a member in Nova Scotia without having to travel; perhaps by way of computers; a special telephone system or something like that. Labeled people will be able to talk to each other without worrying about the cost.

In 1992, Canadian Association for Community Living (CACL) members met with government officials, including Prime Minister Jean Chrétien, to talk about the issues of people with disabilities. I went to represent the International League of Societies for Persons with a Mental Handicap (the ILSMH).

From left to right: Penny Soderena, Harold Barnes, Jean Chretien, and me, Barb Goode.

Many of these organizations are connected. If the CACL was the grandparent, say, then the League would be the great grandparent, I guess. I was involved with so many groups at the time that I was sometimes confused about who I was representing. I still get confused with all the acronyms (names made up of the first letter of each word).

My Goode Home

1992 was also the year I moved to my current home in Burnaby. To me, this move was like a final stepping stone for me in terms of my independence. I had to become completely independent with transit in order to visit my parents. I had to keep to a budget and buy my own groceries; I had to do everything now.

I wanted my full independence, but because I had never had to do some of these things on my own before, I'll admit that it was a little overwhelming at first.

For me, to move from North Vancouver to Burnaby, that was a big leap. A lot people don't think it is, but for me it was. I didn't know Burnaby because I never lived here. I had to learn a lot of new things. And of course, my parents were still living in North Vancouver.

My new home in Burnaby

Part of the reason I moved here was because it was subsidized. It was affordable for me. But at first I thought I made a big mistake moving here, being so far away from my parents.

It would take me one and a half hours to get to Mom and Dad's place on for my Sunday visits. And Dad wanted to give me a ride back, but didn't like driving me all the way home to Burnaby because he was getting older, so he'd drive me halfway home, to the Sea Bus terminal, and I would take transit the rest of the way.

I had been working for the British Columbia Association for Community Living (BCACL) for a long time by then, and a big part of the thing I was doing for BCACL was working with people in Burnaby. So I was lucky in a way – at least I knew a lot of Burnaby people already.

There are 9 suites in my building, and we have all gotten to know each other. But the people here respect each others' privacy; if you don't want to talk to anyone, you don't have to.

When I first moved here, coming up to 20 years ago now and counting, I used to think, I'm not an adult, and this isn't my apartment. I was just looking after it for someone else. It took me a long while to really start feeling like an adult.

I remember being asked, "Barb, what makes you an adult?"

I sat and thought, I don't have a car, and I don't own a home; I don't have a husband or any kids. There are certain things I don't see myself doing that I see "average" people doing.

1992 was a busy year for me, now that I am looking back. Besides the U.N. Conference, the CACL, the BCACL, and my big move, I was also president of the Lower Mainland Community Based Services Society, (LMCBSS) whose first goal, as I already mentioned, was community integration for people moving out of the Woodlands and Glendale Institutions.

CACL sponsored "Independence 1992"; a conference for people with disabilities from all over the world. I put on a day-long seminar on self advocacy. I also did a talk on sterilization without consent.

Some of the other topics at the conference were: education; transportation; and violence. Also: labeling; sharing stories; and inclusion.

We at the LMCBBS started printing a newsletter called the *Community Based Network Newsletter* in April of '92. Two of the themes of the newsletter were the importance of communication and the use of labels.

In the *Community Based Network Newsletter*, we always wrote our articles in clear, plain language, so that everyone could understand.

I had a regular column in the Community Based Network Newsletter called 'Just Ask Barb'. Here's the very first one:

Question – What are self advocates?
Barb – Self advocates are 'mentally challenged' people learning to speak for themselves and fight for their rights.

Question – Do you think that 'mentally challenged' people should live in the community?
Barb – YES I DO! I think 'mentally challenged' people should live in the community like everybody else. For too long, 'mentally challenged' people have had to live in awful places. Why should we have to live in awful places?! Everyone should be treated equally (the same).

By the way, I suppose it goes without saying that I never liked the term mentally challenged either, but it was slightly better than mentally handicapped or mentally retarded, which were the other, even worse labels still regularly used back then.

Me in Amsterdam with Victor, Carol and Robert

I went with a group of six self advocates and six advisors to a conference in Amsterdam. That was in June of 1993. In my travels around the world to different conferences I learned that self advocates everywhere were talking about the same issues.

One issue that we talked about then, and are still talking about today, is labeling. We all want to be people first and not be labeled as retarded or handicapped.

We also talked about how we have a right to make our own decisions and to learn from our own mistakes – like everybody else. It's important to listen to ourselves first instead of always relying on others to make our decisions for us.

The right to vote was another big issue then. In Canada, it hadn't been very long since people with disabilities won the right to vote. But in lots of other countries you lost your rights if you ever lived in an institution, or if you had a guardian – or if you had a label like mentally handicapped or insane.

To this day, many people with disabilities around the world still have no right to vote.

Community Based Network

MARCH, 1993   SUITE 240 LOUGHEED HIGHWAY, BURNABY , B.C.   #10

THE CAMPBELL RIVER SAGA
by Barb Goode and Jack Styan

In October 1993, a group of us (me, Phil Allen and Jack Styan) from the Lower Mainland Community Based Services Society went to Campbell River to put on two presentations about self advocacy. If I remember correctly, the first one was for self advocates from North Island College, and the second was open to anyone.

But the most memorable part of the trip for me was the "wake-up call". You see, Jack wanted a 7 a.m. wake-up call, so I promised that I would phone him. That night there was a BIG storm and all the power went out. It was pitch dark. I woke up during the night to check the time, but the clock was electric and the numbers weren't showing.

I panicked. I tried to phone them, but the phone wouldn't work either.

So I fumbled around in the dark and put my coat on over my pyjamas and pulled my boots on to my bare feet. I couldn't find my glasses, which didn't help at all, believe me.

I went out into the wind and rain. They called it a hotel, but the doors were all outside, like a motel. I tried to figure out where I was going, but there were a lot of doors to other hotel suites, and of course they all looked exactly the same.

I was looking and looking. I knew they were on the same floor as me, but I couldn't remember which door was theirs. So I was just hoping that I would figure out the right one. After walking back and forth forever I finally remembered their suite number.

Hat's off to Phil Allen, Jack Styan and Barb Goode!

A trio of well-known do-"goode"ers: Phil, Jack and Barb

I went to their door and I knocked very lightly. It's a quirk of mine – I don't ever knock loudly and I don't like door bells. Just as I was walking away, Jack finally answered. I told him it was morning, but Jack said, "I don't think so. You should go back to bed."

Phil was still in bed, still

sleeping. We teased him later that during the storm he was dreaming he was in Hawaii.

I went back to my suite after Jack told me to, but I didn't want to oversleep. In any case, I couldn't fall asleep – I was too worried about being late.

By the time morning came, the lights had come back on.

We were prepared to give a big presentation that morning. But first Jack told everyone the story about the power outage and me coming outside in my pyjamas to wake them up in the middle of the night. It could have been 2 or 3 in the morning for all I knew!

Now I know to always bring a watch and a flashlight with me.

> *"We need 4 hugs a day for survival.*
> *We need 8 hugs a day for maintenance.*
> *We need 12 hugs a day for growth."*
>
> Virginia Satir

That same year (1993) I helped the Burnaby Association for the Mentally Handicapped open a subsidized apartment building for independent living. It is not a group home, everyone has their own suite. Some tenants have disabilities, some don't. Some of the people had never lived on their own before. Some of them have never lived away from their families.

I think this kind of housing is helping people to live independently. It's mixed. It's secure. And it's part of the community!

In the October 1993 issue of the Community Based Network newsletter we published a Self Advocates Rights article about having a worker. Here it is.

Stop for a moment and think about Hawaii

"Having a Worker"
By the Editorial Committee

Self Advocate Rights

In July we started talking about rights you have with your worker. We talked about three rights:

1. Right to Power
2. Right to have your own Identity
3. Right to have a say

This month we want to continue talking about rights. Here are three other rights that we think you should have. These three and the three from last month are all from a draft of the Beliefs and Values of the ILSMH. They were written by self advocates and some people who were supporting them.

4) The right to learn. We must take our own risks and learn from our own mistakes.

Parents and helpers often feel we need protection. They feel its their responsibility. That's why they often take over. By doing so, they prevent us from doing things by ourselves. They do not allow us to try, fail and start over again. We don't get the opportunity to learn.

It is important that we be allowed to take our own risks. We want to be prepared to live our own lives. We are willing to learn things. Even it means things will go wrong. Nobody is perfect. By making mistakes and by improving our skills we will grow.

**5) Having the Right to Participate in Community.
People should not be labeled or segregated out of the
mainstream of life.**

Calling us "handicapped" leads to a special circuit of life.
Special day care centres, special schools, special homes
outside community. We are stuck in a circuit that is
outside normal community life. We have less chances to
meet other citizens and exchange ideas. We become
unknown.

We want to join everyone else. We want to be in regular
schools, shops, homes and jobs. We want to be individual
like everyone. Life, we want to be in it.

**6) Being a person. We must be treated as human
beings and as people FIRST**

Other people often notice what we cannot do in the first
place. So others judge us by looking at our disabilities.

We want to emphasize that we are human beings like
others, with abilities and disabilities. And we want to be
respected as persons.

Vol. 1 No. 3

What is "Co-op Housing"?

by Barb Goode

Of course, separately from the Community Based Network newsletter that we were helping to put out for the British Columbia Association for Community Living (BCACL) we self advocates were still publishing our own news-letter – *The Voice.*

Besides travel articles like "My Trip to New Zealand" reprinted here, we talked about self advocates' rights and issues. We wrote articles like "The Right to Vote," and "What is the Residential Tenancy Branch?"

Travels

My Trip to New Zealand

In November (1993), I went to two conferences in New Zealand. The first was in a city called Dunedin. The second conference was in a city called Wellington.

I gave three workshops at the first conference. The first workshop was "Women with Disabilities Talking about Women's Issues". The second was where I talked about a Self Advocates Board that I am on, and I showed a video called "Living with Choices." The third workshop was to the full conference. My topic was "How I see Self Advocacy Going".

At the second conference a friend and I did a session together on "Self Advocacy". When traveling between the two conferences two friends and I talked to different groups of People First.

I spoke about my experience with People First in Canada. It was interesting to know what happens in other countries. In New Zealand, self advocates are on committees that "evaluate" staff. They are also on a committee about sterilization without consent.

I'd like to go back again. I have great memories I'll remember for a long, long time. New Zealand is a beautiful country.

One of the other things that we did in *The Voice* newsletter was to keep people with disabilities informed about laws that affected them. In the same issue that my article about New Zealand was published, we ran an article about the changing guardianship rules.

At that time, we at the B.C. Self Advocacy Caucus had just put out a plain language pamphlet on Guardianship. Because the recent changes to guardianship laws gave people with guardians or trustees more choices in their lives, we felt that it was important to tell other self advocates about it.

Diane Marleau Minister of Health presents Norm Goode with Canada Volunteer Award

Dad won the Canada Volunteer Award in 1993 for his 30 years of volunteer service.

It turned out that Dad's Canada Volunteer Award was the same award that I had won back in 1987. But Dad's award came with a medal and mine didn't, so it took us a while to realize that it was the same award.

Dad volunteered many years for the North Shore Association for the Mentally Handicapped, and at least twelve years with POLARIS Employment Services Society, including eight years as President of the Board. POLARIS helps people with disabilities to find meaningful paid work.

Even though he did all that volunteer work, he never saw himself as a leader. When he was asked about his Canada Volunteer Award after the presentation, he said very quietly, "Other people in the field deserve this award as much or more than I do."

Dad fought in the Second World War and won four medals, but he never picked them up. He said he didn't deserve them; he was just doing what any soldier would do. Many years later, my Mom checked on the medals, and the army still had them. And so she got them to send the medals to Dad. When he got them he mounted them on a nice board, and he left them to me when he passed away.

People often say I am humble, well, I guess I get that from my Dad. He always used to tell me, "You don't show people you can do something by talking about it; you show them you can do it by doing it."

I remember Mom and Dad had a problem with squirrels getting into the house. Dad would never hurt a living thing, so he would catch the squirrels, put them in a cage, and then drive out to the park where he liked to walk. I asked him whether it helped to drive the squirrels all the way out to the park. He shrugged and said, "No, they always follow me home."

As I mentioned already, in the early to mid-1990's, the years leading up to the final closure of British Columbia's institutions for people with mental handicaps, I was

Dad's friend.

involved with the British Columbia Association for Community Living (BCACL). One of our goals, at that time, was to try to make sure that housing, job training, jobs, and access to doctors and dentists in the community were all in place for people before they moved into the community.

We were somewhat successful with housing, doctors, and dentists, but there ended up being very few job opportunities for people with disabilities coming into the community. Unfortunately, this is still true today.

In an early 1990's issue of the BCACL's Community Living News my friend Fred Ford wrote about Women's History Month. In his article he paid me a great compliment by honouring my work for women (and men) with disabilities. He wrote:

> *Barb Goode is a woman who has had a major impact on the disability rights movement. In 1985, Barb led a group of self advocates (the Consumer Advisory Committee) in attaining intervener status in the landmark 'Eve' Case, concerning the sterilization of a PEI woman.*

> *Barb led this fight to the Supreme Court of Canada when national and provincial advocacy organizations were unable to reach a consensus on the issue. The Supreme Court concurred with Barb's group's position and affirmed the right of people with mental handicaps to be protected from non-therapeutic sterilizations.*

Barb has been involved as a project coordinator and as co-author in a number of projects and publications related to the rights of people with disabilities, including "The Right to Control what Happens to your Body."

On October 12, 1992, Barb became the first self advocate to speak to the General Assembly of the United Nations in New York City. At the first International People First conference, held in June of 1993 in Toronto, Barb was the recipient of the first International Self Advocacy Award – this award was named in honour of Rosemary Dybwad, herself a tireless advocate for the rights of people with disabilities. Barb was given this award in recognition of her leadership in the self advocacy movement locally, nationally, and internationally. Currently, Barb is a member of the International League of Societies for Persons with a Mental Handicap.

It is the not-so-everyday rebellions waged by people like Barb Goode that quietly change the world.

By 1993, when the ILSMH met in Holland, there were representatives from Germany, Australia, New Zealand and Sweden. In Holland, we (the self advocates) ran our own small conference at the same time the League held their meetings. Our small group of self advocates spent quite a bit of time planning for our next conference. We wanted to make sure there were even more self advocates getting involved.

And there were. At the next conference in India there were around 60 self advocates from all over the world, but I was still the only one from Canada.

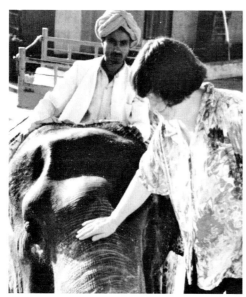

My Jumbo Buddy

In New Delhi we discussed discrimination, women's issues, housing, how to run meetings, and what the role of self advocates should be in helping other self advocates. Some of these sessions were long, because some people needed to have their languages translated, and we had to make sure to use plain language so that everyone there could understand.

At the India conference, we learned that many people from the poorer countries had never met another self advocate in their whole lives. And their staff were more likely to speak for them, instead of assisting them to speak for themselves. It was harder to get their support staff to translate exactly what the person was saying and not to speak for them. This is a problem in Canada too, and other countries, but there was a noticeable difference with the people from third world countries. Some self advocates seemed almost afraid to say what they really felt, because their staff were always right there with them.

It made me smile when a few days into the conference some of the self advocates from poorer countries came in with t-shirts on that said "Self Advocates!" They had just learned what self advocacy was all about and they were so proud that they went out and had the t-shirts made.

We planned for the next meeting which took place in 1996 in Chile. For the meeting in Chile we had decided to keep in touch directly, rather than always going through the ILSMH head office in Belgium. So it was easier for us to be prepared for Chile.

In Chile, I met a man who looked exactly like Robin Williams! He didn't speak English and I didn't speak his language, but we still got along great. We became goode friends and we even went skiing together while I was there. Imagine – skiing in Chile! Well, you learn something new every day, and one thing I learned on that trip is that Chile is one of the favourite skiing destinations in the entire southern hemisphere.

> *Nurture your mind with great thoughts.*
> Benjamin Disraeli

Also in 1996, as outgoing president of the Lower Mainland Community Based Services Society, I was active in developing Ridgeview Heights, a mixed use affordable housing complex for seniors, low income families and folks with disabilities. The complex also includes space for community-based services such as a neighborhood house and continuing education classes.

So, after my trip to Chile my focus shifted back home. I traveled less internationally, but much more within British Columbia and Canada. As I mentioned, I worry about international travel, so I really don't mind working closer to home.

Speaking at a conference in Jamaica

Sometime, in amongst all that traveling, I also went to Mexico and Jamaica.

In the late 1990's I was part of a project called So Far. This project was sponsored by the British Columbia Association for Community Living and many other organizations and individuals.

In this project, a few people with disabilities, myself included, were taught writing and literacy skills. By the end we had each done an interview and written a story, which ended up in a book called *So Far: Words From Learners*. It was a great idea for a project – nothing like it had ever been done before, as far as I know – but now that I read over my contribution, it makes me quite emotional.

You see, my interview and my writing project were both about my first cat, Cuddles Snuggles (or C.S. if I was too embarrassed to tell someone her real name). And Cuddles Snuggles was killed by a car just as the book was being sent to the printer.

In my interview and in my story I talked about how long I had to think before finally deciding to get a pet. I was comparing my own growing independence to the idea of having a living creature who would totally depend on me.

Another tough thing was that I was unemployed at the time the So Far project was happening. I was looking hard for a clerical job, but without much luck. I had at least half a dozen volunteer jobs, but I was always worried about money and paying my bills.

I believe in volunteering, and I think that everyone should get involved and volunteer for something they believe in. I think all employed or unemployed people with disabilities should volunteer. It makes a positive difference in the

world and it makes the volunteers feel goode about themselves. Every single person has the ability to help out in some way. Everyone has gifts to share.

Of course, you should still keep looking for paid work; after all, we all have our bills to pay. But don't frown on volunteering.

Quite a while later, I adopted Sante Claws.

The 2000's

"It's Not What We Give..."

> *A Daily Affirmation:*
> *'It's not what we give, but what we get in return for caring that matters.'*

I guess in the last five or ten years I've finally started to see myself as an adult. Like I said, I always saw myself as a child. And it's really strange; I can never understand for the life of me why adults with disabilities are so often treated like children. I think if I had been treated like an adult more often, I might have felt more like an adult.

A friend of mine – he's in his late 50's and he's still at home. He has a disability and his mom wants him at home, and I can understand that. I really can. But I worry about what will happen when his mom is gone. He has never had to learn to be independent, so it will be hard for him.

I think that other people sometimes believe that if you're not married with kids, if you don't have a car, if you don't have a job fulltime, if you don't have anything worth a lot of money, then you shouldn't be treated as an adult.

Personally, I never got someone else to buy me anything. Mom and Dad always told me that if you buy it yourself then it's really yours. The things I have are the things that make me happy; things like pictures, and this may seem funny, but a fuzzy blanket. It may not be much, but I worked for what I have, and I bought it all myself. I've never taken out a loan or used credit.

I am feeling like I can be myself now more than ever. My parents' generation thought that people should dress properly – to fit in. But I can't help it, I like to stand out.

I remember back when I was in my early 20's my friend wanted to cut my hair short, then she wanted me to dress in a poncho and a bright dress. So, I did. And I liked it.

My parents weren't too sure. When they first saw me they didn't even know who I was....

For me, the 2000's have gone by in the snap of a finger. I think I probably averaged one or two workshops or conferences per month all the way through that decade. I have been asked to do more and more presentations as well over the years, which I often do with other self advocates and friends.

I have worked at Polaris Employment Services Society for more than ten years; the same Polaris that my Dad volunteered so many years for.

Polaris assists people with disabilities to find and keep real and meaningful jobs. They help folks make, and complete, action plans. An action plan could include making a job choice, skills training, job searching, and job keeping.

> *"Our hearts are next door neighbours, although our homes are miles apart."*
> *Anonymous*

Another thing that stands out for me about the 2000's is that for the last few years I have been a reporter for *The Citizen*, the CLBC newsletter. It all started at a Community Living British Columbia (CLBC) staff conference. I was asked to attend in the role of roving reporter. What I was asked to do was to go around and ask random staff a few questions.

STAFF CONFERENCE: A SELF-ADVOCATE'S PERSPECTIVE
By Barb Goode, *roving reporter, also known as ice-cream cone*

I attended the second CLBC Staff Conference. I was asked for the second year running to be a roving reporter. At the last conference, Penny from Prince George and I asked staff a question and at the end of the conference we reported back the top nine responses.

This year, we asked the question with our new reporter Gladys, "How can we become a learning organization?" A friend of mine helped me. I asked the question and she wrote down the answers. Penny taped her responses and someone typed it up for her. Gladys did it her way – I don't know how she did it. I think it's okay to do it different.

The staff were interested and very helpful when I interviewed them. I was glad we were introduced on Monday morning so staff knew who we were and what we were doing.

I was glad they got papers in their packages to think about and fill out.

I attended some of the workshops. They were very interesting. There were so many workshops to choose from. I liked a lot of the workshop's names. There were different workshops, like one called "Listen! Listen! Listen!" that self advocates put on, and another one was on work. There were other ones too.

On Monday night there was a dinner and dance. After the dinner, there was an awards presentation given to seven self-advocates

(back row, from left): Richard McDonald; Ludo Van Pelt; Gerry Jozsmas; Tom Christensen, Minister of Children and Family Development. (front row, from left): Darryl Harauc; Penny Soderena; Shelley Marimus; Barb Goode; Lois Hollstedt, CLBC Board of Directors Chair

called the Lifetime Achievement Award. I was one of the lucky ones. I was very honoured and touched.

It was great to see friends again. Some of the staff got an award also. That is such a cool idea. And there was a cool picture show at the end.

It was a very good conference. I enjoyed it all.

A staff member from Burnaby Association for Community Inclusion (BACI) had the job of writing down the answers for me, because I found it hard to remember everything that everyone had said. My partner and I got together after the interviews and summarized all the answers, and at the end of the day we did a presentation on our findings.

The next year I was invited back again as roving reporter. This time, there was another roving reporter who was recording her interviews on a tape recorder. Since I can't stand hearing my voice on tape, I stuck with my original method of enlisting a partner.

By the end of the conference we were all getting tired and we started fooling around. I took the microphone and went up to someone as if I was going to interview them, but I stumbled when I got up to them and the microphone fell on the floor.

I cried, "I dropped my ice cream cone!" and everyone laughed.

So now, whenever I put on my reporter's hat, my nickname is Ice Cream Cone.

I have been taking reading and writing classes for the last several years as well. The most recent one is run kind of like a book club. My current teacher's name is Merrilyn Cook. She is one of the best teachers I have ever had, and I feel like I've learned a lot from her. She is patient and she gives her students time to think things through.

Me, Merrilyn Cook, and two of my classmates, Angie and Lisa.

Another favourite teacher of mine (who is now my goode friend) is Maureen Olofson.

Education is so important, and we all learn in different ways.

This is something that we are talking about more these days. I feel that people with disabilities should always be included and involved in learning new things.

If we can find the right teachers, we can learn anything! We all have had teachers who have been important to us in our lives. And the reason they have been so important is because they teach us in ways that we understand best.

109

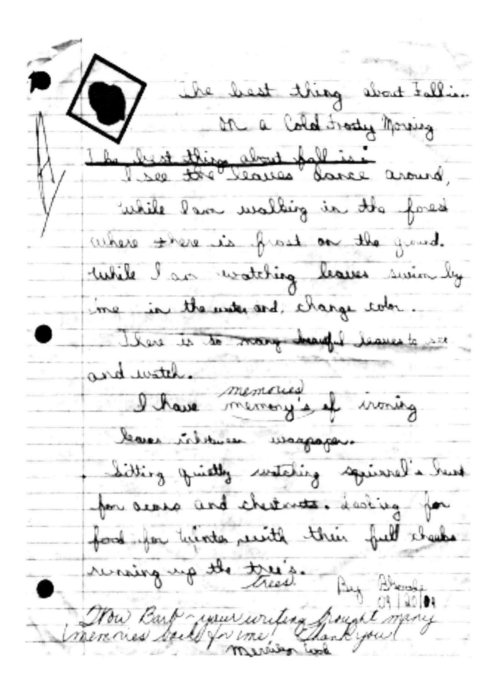

The best thing about Fall is..
In a Cold frosty Morning
The best thing about fall is:
I see the leaves dance around,
while I am walking in the forest
where there is frost on the ground.
While I am watching leaves swim by
me in the water and, change color.
There is so many beautiful leaves to see
and watch.
I have memories of ironing
leaves between waxpaper.
Sitting quietly watching squirrel's hunt
for acorns and chestnuts. looking for
food for winter with their full cheeks
running up the trees.
By Brenda
09/20/09

Now Burt - your writing brought many
memories back for me! Thank you!
Marilyn

Me in Paris with my
friends
Andre and Gayle

In 2006, Jack Styan, executive director of the Planned Lifetime Advocacy Network (PLAN), nominated me for the W. J. Van Dusen Community Service Award. I am so thankful to him for this. Here is part of the flattering nomination letter he wrote. Jack is a goode friend of mine, and I am very proud of this award.

". . . Barb has inspired a generation of persons with developmental disabilities and redefined how we look at disability. She has influenced and given hope to thousands of families.

I have known Barb for nearly 20 years. Barb is my only friend that has addressed the General Assembly of the United Nations and spoken at conferences in places like New Dehli, Finland, Africa and Chile, among others. More than anyone I know, Barb has dedicated her life to building a stronger, healthier community.

Barb is one of the mothers of the "self advocacy" movement in Canada. Her work in provincial, national and international arenas with B.C. Association for Community Living, Canadian

Association for Community Living and Inclusion International, over the past 25 years has inspired thousands of persons with disabilities around B.C., across Canada and around the world to speak out for themselves and to organize to gain strength by uniting.

. . .

If you were to meet Barb you couldn't differentiate her from the many other people you might meet in a day. However, hidden behind her unassuming and humble nature is a deep strength and a powerful commitment to creating a better world. Irrespective of recognition or appreciation, Barb keeps giving and giving and giving, making her home, her organizations and her community warmer, kinder places to be.

. . .

My PATH – 2009

I had been to friends' PATH meetings many times before, but I had never had one of my own. PATH stands for Planning Alternative Tomorrows with Hope. It is a life-planning tool that was developed by Jack Pierpont, Marsha Forest, Judith Snow and John O'Brien.

I was actually a bit nervous when I had the chance to have a planning meeting like this. What would my future look like?

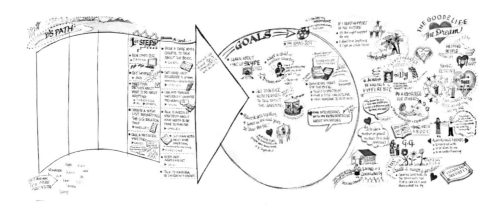

My PATH, just before it was completed...

My friend Shelley Nessman was the facilitator and the amazing artist Avril Orloff was the graphic recorder who drew my beautiful PATH.

The whole process worked out really well! As a group we kind of brainstormed ideas of what I wanted to see happen in my life. People in my network gave me suggestions, too. By the end I had some immediate goals to work on and a few ideas for some future plans.

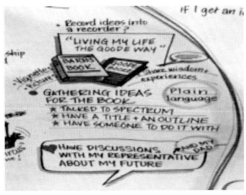

2009 PATH goal. Dreams can come true!

Some ideas we came up with were for me to

become a foster-child parent to a child in another country, to make a memory garden for my Mom and Dad, and to write my own book. There were other things too, but these three were the biggest ideas.

In some ways I felt like I was seeing my life in a different way – IN A "GOODE" WAY!

Afterwards, we had a great pot luck dinner. I have already achieved some of my goals, as you know, because here you are reading my book!

Dad

When I was a kid, I remember that Dad made his own beer. But especially in his last few years, Dad loved having his beer. If he missed that, it wasn't goode. One day he went out for lunch with my cousin to their usual place, and he ordered a beer like he always did.

The waiter said, "I'm sorry sir, we don't sell beer any longer."

Dad got up and walked out.

Another time, Dad had an appointment at the dentist. They called and asked him to come in a little early, but then they kept him waiting for over an hour.

Dad missed his beer with my cousin. He was upset with the dentist, not for keeping him waiting, but for making him miss his beer.

Now

In the 1990's and 2000's I talked a lot about equal rights for people with disabilities, but right now I'm talking more about accessibility.

Part of the recent talk about accessibility is around email, the internet, and social networking websites and how to use these things safely.

Recently, Facebook and other social networking websites are being used to help people with disabilities stay connected to their networks. But people need to be taught how to use the internet safely.

Everyone should take a course on internet safety before they start using these websites. If someone has staff helping them, they should take a course together.

Accessibility is also about transportation, education, money, job availability, and so much more; it's about people with disabilities having the opportunity to make a wide range of choices like everyone else.

I wholeheartedly agree with a friend of mine who once said to me, "Language needs a ramp, like wheelchairs do, to be accessible." So, as you can probably tell, plain language is still very important to me. I have worked on many plain language projects over the years and continue to do so.

To this day, it upsets me that so many of the official forms that people with disabilities have in their lives are very complicated. Just the other day I got a very confusing three page government letter. Even with a friend to help me, it took us a while to figure out that there was just one simple question they were asking.

Another focus of mine right now is poverty. I would like to see people with disabilities living above the poverty line. This means better benefits for people who need them, and it also means access to real and meaningful employment.

I am glad to see that more importance is being put on friendships. I am really glad about this, because it is maybe the biggest issue for people with disabilities – that so many don't have any unpaid friends. All people with disabilities should be getting out regularly and meeting new people, and connecting, or re-connecting with their families. We all need to have a network of unpaid friends and family who will be there for us in our times of need (and, of course, when we want to celebrate).

It takes work (having a personal support network) on both parts. Staff can be the roadblocks. Not always, but often. Because staff say they want people to have friendships, but they don't always truly support it or mean it. Sometimes, well-meaning staff don't know how to get out of the way, or they don't want to look like they are not doing their jobs properly.

As self advocates, we talk a lot these days about how to help other folks with disabilities to become the leaders of their own support networks. Through Community Living B.C. I've been going around the Province with a group doing People Planning Together training, where we help people to make hopeful plans for a happy life.

The People Planning Together workshops made those of us working on it think about branching out into workshops about improving self esteem, loneliness, and focusing on our gifts.

I find that one of the biggest problems facing people with disabilities today is their reluctance to get involved in working for their rights. Really, it has been a problem since day one.

Actually, maybe reluctance is the wrong word to use. After all, many of the people with disabilities who have not been involved in working for their rights have never been asked to get involved. They don't necessarily know how to do it, or even where to begin. As well, some people still feel like they are not *allowed* to get involved. To my mind, this is the kind of damage that the institutions have done. And even in some of the group homes today they don't encourage the people they support to speak up for themselves, or to make friends outside the home.

It is time for everyone to support all people with disabilities to be the leaders of their own lives and to enjoy the rights and responsibilities of full inclusion in society.

We need to continue to speak up for our rights in order to protect them. We should never forget the horrors of the institutions, because if we do, we risk going back in time to the warehousing of "problem" human beings in prison- or hospital-like settings – without a thought for their feelings, and with no use for their gifts.

It is up to *all of us* to continue to teach everyone in our communities that folks with disabilities have the same rights as everyone else. No matter how long it might take for some people to learn, the end result is rewarding for the whole society.

Maybe a goode example of what I am talking about is this: that even though we won the "Eve" case way back in 1986, I am still concerned about sterilization of people with disabilities. If it is still happening somewhere in the world (and it is, believe me), it is still a problem, and so people need to keep working on making it right.

Basically, now that I think about it, I am worried about all the same things I have been worried about all my life.
But, in any case, I guess I'll just continue to take my parents' advice to believe in myself and just keep on going.

In a recent interview for the Community Living B.C. magazine The Citizen, here is what I said, *"I don't want to be a token member (of my six current volunteer committees), just being quiet and looking pretty. I want to be involved. I never want to retire."*

> *"Flowers are sunshine, food, and medicine to the soul."*
> Luther Burbank

*"We've been talking about some of these issues for so long,
it seems like we'll still be talking about them
'til the cows come home." Barb*

Labels and Double Standards

I printed and saved this article by my friend Al Etmanski about the 2010 Paralympic Games opening ceremonies that I attended with him. The article addresses the issue of labeling and includes some information about the "Eve" Case. Here it is:

I sat with Barb Goode during the Paralympic opening ceremonies last Friday. As tributes were paid to Terry Fox and Rick Hansen, I couldn't help but reflect on Barb's pioneering role in breaking stereotypes towards people who are labeled mentally handicapped and the unfairness that so few knew about her when the barriers she faced were as formidable as Terry and Rick faced. In some ways the obstacles she has overcome and is still confronting are more insidious because they can't be fixed with a wheelchair, a ramp, or a prosthetic.

Within the hierarchy of disability Barb is dealing with the least understood and the most underappreciated – developmental disability.

In fact, when she started her career as an advocate people used deeply offensive words, like retarded and moron. That these terms are no longer in common usage can be linked to Barb's leadership.

Barb has been proving people wrong for decades. She considers herself an advocate, which means you want her on your side if you are fighting for your rights. She was one of twelve Canadians organizing among folks with disabilities. In 1986 Barb Goode led the Supreme Court intervention in the case of Eve. The subsequent Supreme Court decision prevents the sterilization if people with intellectual disabilities for non-medical reasons.

Given Canada's sad history of enforced sterilization of people with intellectual disabilities Barb's intervention is a milestone on par with recognizing the damages of residential schools for Aboriginal children or the internment of Japanese Canadians.

In 1992 she became the first person with a disability to address the U.N. General Assembly. Many would consider that the peak of their career. Barb, of course, doesn't see it this way. If you ask her for the highlights of her advocacy career she will say, "Meeting so many interesting people." Like many effective leaders, it is her relationships that define Barb. She is the ultimate networker – her address

book contains more entries than anyone I know.

She is self-effacing to a fault. And eternally vigilant. When she reads this she will gently scold me to use plain language. And that is why the B.C. Representative Agreement Act is noteworthy not only for its progressive content, but also for being readable to non-lawyers and lay people. You can thank Barb for the move to plain language legislation in British Columbia.

She sums up her career as, "Doing things people didn't think I could." That's clearly the message of the Vancouver Paralympic Games. As you watch the closing ceremonies tonight, spare a thought for one of the foremost builders of the modern day disability movement. A hero who deserves to be included in the same breath as Terry Fox and Rick Hansen.

Changes in Labels over the Years

Defective became insane became retarded became mentally retarded became mentally handicapped became mentally challenged became developmentally delayed became intellectually challenged became people with mental handicaps became people with disabilities. See how long it took for people to come before disability.

Oh, I know I'm leaving out lots of other negative labels, but I think my point is clear: it is a slow process getting people to change their habits; getting people to think in terms of people first, not disability first; to think in terms of gifts instead of challenges.

I used to prefer "community living people," but now I like "people with diversibilities."

Here are some of the associations that I have been involved with and the name changes they have gone through.

The Canadian Association for Community Living used to be called the Canadian Association for the Mentally Retarded.

The British Columbia Association for Community Living was called British Columbians for Mentally Handicapped People. It was originally called the British Columbia Association for the Mentally Retarded.

The International League of Persons with a Mental Handicap is now known as Inclusion International.

Burnaby Association for the Mentally Handicapped is now called the Burnaby Association for Community Inclusion.

North Shore Connexions used to be called The North Shore Association for the Mentally Retarded.

Some people complain that it is confusing to have to deal with so many name changes. The people who complain, I have noticed, are people who are generally not labeled by their disabilities. If they were, I am sure they would see it differently.

"M.R. stands for Mighty Remarkable"

Barb Goode

I often talk about "double standards". Part of what I mean by this is how I am sometimes treated like an adult and sometimes treated like a child. All people with divers-ibilities go through this.

Many years ago I wrote this article for *The Voice*, "Double Standards":

> It has been a concern of mine for a long time that Self Advocates are treated differently than other people. This is called double standards.

> I have one example of many that have happened to me.

I was at a conference and was visiting a gardening site of a local association. A staff was showing me and another Self Advocate around and we were taking a break when we were asked to sit with the other staff who were having coffee.

I felt very uncomfortable because of two things. One being this friend who is a self advocate and I were asked to sit with the other staff but other self advocates who were there were not.

A the table with the other staff we were not talked to so I got up and left to talk to other Self Advocates in another room.

And also there was a woman Self Advocate that told me something.

She turned around and told the staff the same thing and they told her to wait till later.   The staff told her to "go away" but when I wanted to tell them something they didn't tell me to "go away."

One of the problems was that I didn't know if it was all in my imagination.

The main concern I have is how to deal with it. Knowing how to deal with it and knowing that it is wrong.   Also how to explain it to other Self Advocates.

How do you tell someone this is how you're treating me and this is how I'm feeling.   If you have

experiences or ideas about how to deal with this let
me know.

In a more recent example I went to visit family from out of town one weekend. My family didn't want me to use transit there on my own. They presumed that I couldn't do it.

I know they just wanted to protect me, but here in Vancouver I am someone that people come to when they want to know which buses to take. I have become an expert because I never had a car, and I had to learn how to get around all over the place on my own. I know how to read a bus schedule and I am not afraid to ask for directions.

I mean, I managed to find my way around Nairobi, New Delhi, Amsterdam, New York, and many other places around the world. I'm sure I could find my way around anywhere.

I have to keep remembering to have faith in myself in the face of obstacles, even (or especially) when people tell me I can't do things that I know I can do. I try to remember to take every opportunity to teach the people who worry too much about me that there is dignity in taking risks.

YOU AND I

by Elaine Popovich

I am a resident. You reside.
I am admitted. You move in.

I am aggressive. You are assertive.

I have behavior problems. You are rude.

I am noncompliant. You don't like being told what to do.

When I ask you out for dinner, it is an outing. When you ask someone out, it is a date.

I made mistakes during my check-writing program. Some day I might get a bank account. You forgot to record some withdrawals from your account. The bank called to remind you.

I wanted to talk with the nice-looking person behind us at the grocery store. I was told that it is inappropriate to talk to strangers. You met your spouse in the produce department. Neither of you could find the bean sprouts.

I celebrated my birthday yesterday with five other residents and two staff members. I hope my family sends a card. Your family threw you a surprise party. Your brother couldn't make it from out of state. It sounded wonderful!

My case manager sends a report every month to my guardian. It says everything I did wrong and some things I did right. You are still mad at your sister for calling your Mom after you got that speeding ticket.

I am learning household skills. You hate housework.

I am learning leisure skills. Your shirt says you are a "Couch Potato."

After I do my budget program tonight, I might get to go to McDonald's if I have enough money. You were glad that the new French restaurant took your charge card.

My case manager, psychologist, R. N., occupational and physical therapist, nutritionist and house staff set

goals for me for the next year. You haven't decided
what you want out of life.
Someday I will be discharged . . . maybe. You will
move onward and upward.

Another thing, I don't like how there are getting to be all these distinctions between disabilities. We have gone from people with disabilities to people with autism, or Asperger's, or fetal alcohol syndrome, or whatever. To my way of thinking, these new labels are just as harmful as the old ones. They focus on problems instead of strengths, and they are used as excuses for why labeled people are not allowed to do things that other people can do; why they cannot have the same variety of choices that other people do.

I sometimes ask people without disabilities to think about whether they would like to be known as people with diabetes or people with heart disease; people with deafness or depression – you get the picture. And do you know what they almost always say? They say, "No, my medical information is personal. It is strictly between me and my doctor, and maybe some family members or close friends."

That is my point. Nobody wants to be known for their shortcomings. Negative labels limit people. If we labeled people for their strengths, wouldn't they be more likely to succeed in life?

We are all put here on earth for a reason. Don't you think so? And don't you think that our lives should be spent looking for and sharing our gifts – in other words, finding and sharing our reason for being here in the first place?

For me it's one of the biggest issues, the negative labels people put on other people.

For me, labels extend to the assumptions people make about me over the telephone. Sometimes when I answer the phone people will say: "Oh... is your mother home?" That really gets to me. They think I'm a little kid because of the way my voice sounds. Sometimes, if I am feeling cheeky, I say, "Just a minute..." and I leave the phone and come back and say, "I'm sorry. My Mom's not home right now. Can I help you?" ☺ These days I say, "My mother asked me to find out what this call is about."

Pretending

Not too long ago, my friend Shelley Nessman and I were out on this call together and I was asked a question like, "Do people ever treat you differently because you don't appear to be handicapped?" And I said, "My concern is that because I don't appear to be disabled that some people think I'm pretending I'm disabled." Shelley jokingly said that I should reply with something like, "Are you

> "What gets to me is I'm told sometimes that I'm pretending to be handicapped ... to me that's an insult."
>
> *A quote of mine from*
> *The Vancouver Sun*

pretending to be normal?" Of course, Shelley knows that I am not a very sarcastic person by nature, and I would never really say anything like that.

I emailed Shelley once about pretending. We were going to be doing a talk on the subject. I wrote:

"All my life, but especially in the past two years, people have said that I am pretending to be disabled. It is very hurtful to me. Sometimes I really do think about saying, "Are you pretending to be normal?" Some of my friends with disabilities have told me that people have told them the same thing. I feel everyone has a quirk of some kind. This is a very sensitive subject for me.

Guess Who!!

"We are all people trying the best we can. Love yourself and take one day at a time. Take one minute at a time or whatever you wish."

Shelley wrote back:

"It doesn't matter if people think you're pretending. That's their problem. You don't need to explain. You know who you are. The expert on your life is YOU!"

I wrote her back:

"Shelley, you always make me feel wunderbar – and "goode" about myself!"

133

The 2010s? or What Does the Future Hold?

> *"Grow old along with me!*
> *The best is yet to be,*
> *The last of life,*
> *For which the first was made."*
>
> Robert Browning

My Dream House:

I loved the bathtub that was in my first apartment. It had claw feet. Oh yes, I love those old bathtubs. But to get in and out you needed a ladder, or at least a step stool.... The other thing that apartment had was lots of cupboard space in the kitchen.

In my own mind I have always pictured that I want for my dream place to be the best things from all the places I have ever lived.

My third or fourth apartment was a basement suite with a really big bedroom. I would keep the bathroom from the first place and the bedroom from this other one. There was another place I lived that had a kitchen I would keep part of, because it was huge and had so much counter space and a big window that looked out to a courtyard, and that was really neat.

And my dream place would have big living room windows too, so that when I looked outside, I could see my beautiful garden.

I would like to face the mountains, and have a creek nearby. That part would be from my Mom and Dad's old place, because when I was growing up in North Vancouver, we lived at the foot of a mountain, with a creek running past the back yard.

I would always want to be on the ground floor with a back and front entrance and plenty of space for a garden. Perhaps it would just be a short stroll to the beach!

The bridge along my dream path to the beach.

Getting Prepared for Aging with Hope

I've always been afraid to show strong emotions; afraid that someone will think I'm out of control and want to lock me up. As I said before, being forced to move to a facility is one of my greatest fears.

And I'm lucky. Even though some people suggested that an institution would be the best place for me, my parents always said no. "Barb will be fine living at home with us."

I know I'm repeating myself here, but when I was a little kid, some people told my parents that we should move to Victoria, because they thought the institution there was better than Woodlands. This advice made my Dad quite upset, I remember.

My fear of institutionalization is even worse now that my parents have passed away. But, I fear it much more-so for my friends and other people with disabilities who did have to live in institutions. They are terrified of having to go back.

My message is: be prepared. Make sure your wishes for how you want to end your life are understood, and that you have people in your life who will be there to make sure that your wishes are fulfilled.

I'm afraid for people living in group homes, especially the people with communication challenges; afraid that their wishes won't be understood or fulfilled. If you ask me, I would say that none of the people who began their lives in an institution would want to finish their lives in another institution. Everyone wants to die with dignity.

It is hard for me to talk about this, but I saw my own Mom go into a seniors' facility and die there. She was always so independent; she would even argue with me when I would tease her that her poor vision was a disability.

I know my Mom would never have chosen to end her life in a facility like she did. A lot of people are just not prepared.

I have a representation agreement and a will. If I am unable to look after my own money or health issues, I have legal paperwork in place so that my wishes will be fulfilled, and I have friends that will help me. One of the most important things for me is to stay at home – not to go into a facility.

> *"Worry is like a rocking chair, it gives you something to do but it gets you nowhere."*
> Anonymous
> *(corny, but true)*

Here is a 1994 interview I did:

Interviewer: What is your vision of life in the 21st century for people with disabilities?

Barb: Well, to see all people with friends, living in the community, with the supports they need... Everyone working together... A world where people help each other out... Having jobs, raising families... Where people are respected for who they are and what they can do even if they need help.

Interviewer: A world where we don't need labels but where we simply ask how we can help?

Barb: How we can help each other.

Tuesday November 2nd, 2010
I got engaged to a great
wonderful Man. His name
Is Harold Barnes. We have
known each other 27 years
++. Now I have to think
about 2 of us. He is from
Red Deer Alberta. Now we
can grow old together.

Yes, it's true! The love of my life asked me to marry him. We were at a conference in Ottawa. I wrote this note to myself as soon as I got back to my hotel room.

Here I am with Harold at a recent National Family Conference in Whistler Village, British Columbia. Did I mention that he is the love of my life?

Mom's Spicy Spaghetti

1 teaspoon cooking oil

1 pound ground beef

1 onion chopped

1 large can of tomatoes

1 teaspoon minced garlic

8 fresh mushrooms, sliced

1 stick of celery and 1 carrot, chopped

2 teaspoons Italian seasoning

1/2 teaspoon dried chili flakes (if you like it spicy)

1 small jar tomato paste

Noodles

Parmesan cheese

1 tablespoon parsley

Put meat, onion and garlic together into a large pan with the oil. Add chopped vegetables. Add tomatoes, Italian seasoning and chilli flakes. Cook over low heat one hour. Add the tomato paste at the end to thicken. Add salt and pepper to taste.

Cook over low heat for 15 minutes before the sauce is ready, cook noodles in boiling water to desired softness. Place noodles on the plate, spoon over some sauce and sprinkle with parsley and parmesan cheese.

10 Questions

At Vancouver's 2010 Community Living Month "Celebration of Stories in Community Living," hosted by Vela Microboard Association, Spectrum Society and the 101 Friends Project, Jim Reynolds and I prepared a Question and Answer presentation on my process of writing this book. Here it is exactly as we prepared it:

10 Questions About Writing Her Memoirs

Disability rights and self advocate leader Barb Goode is in the process of writing her memoirs.

If anything doesn't make sense to you during this present-ation, please stop us and ask.

1) What made you decide to write a book?
"I originally thought of just making 5 copies for friends – those first five could lend it to 5 others, and so on....
"Many people have told me to write about the disability rights movement from my way of thinking"

2)   What are some of the important ideas you discuss in your book?
"Labels, double standards . . .
"The importance of friendships versus staff relationships – meaning unpaid versus paid friendships . . .
"It's not disabilities anymore, it's diversibilities . . .
"Equality – (equal rights for people with diversibilities) - same status, same rights for everyone . . .

"Plain language/accessibility - easy access for all . . ."

3)   Who will you dedicate your book to?
"Mom and Dad (buy my book and you will see why) ☺ *..."*

4)   What do you hope your readers will learn from your book?
"That people will be more understanding in the way they treat labeled people - labels stick with people for life, we are people first . . .
"That it's important to keep fighting for equality for folks with diversibilities . . ."

5)   What have the challenges been for you in writing your book?
"Bringing up some not-so-good memories and emotions (For example, I feel upset that my Mom and Dad won't see my book) Dad would have liked it; Mom – I don't know – she didn't always understand the things I did, but I know she would have been proud of me in her own way . . .
"I'm concerned that readers won't understand why I wrote the book, and that they might think I have a 'big head' . . .
"I have feelings of insecurity about the book being interesting and informative . . .
"It is overwhelming to sit and write a book. There are many ways to do it. I got a tape recorder, because people told me that it would make it easier for me, but it wasn't. I don't like hearing my own voice on tape. Having someone to help allows me to bounce off ideas and get my thoughts into some kind of order and to help me get through some of the less comfortable topics. It was important for me to find someone to help me who gets what I am saying and who won't

change things into their words instead of mine – someone who encourages me."

6)   What advice do you have for other folks with disabilities / diversibilities who might want to write a book?

"If I can write a book, so can anybody else who has a story to tell and the excitement to tell it . . .

"As I said, bring in people to help you, but don't let them change it into their words instead of your own . . .

"It is not a failure to ask for help - as I found out . . ."

7)   Is there still work to be done in the diversibility / disability rights movement?

"Yes, there will always be more work to be done . . .

"It's important to keep reminding people in a gentle way that people with diversibilities have rights too . . ."

8)   What is a self advocate and why is important to be one?

"Self advocates are people with diversibilities learning to speak for ourselves, taking control of our own lives, and working for our rights . . .

"It is important to keep reminding people about the rights and equality that we have all worked so hard for. Without new leaders joining the self advocacy movement, we could easily lose the rights that we have gained. It is important to keep moving (forward) . . ."

With David Pitonyak as we prepare for our presentations at the Celebration of Stories

9)   What do you think is the most important issue facing self advocates today as we get older?

"The backslide, or what I call going back in time and losing our rights . . .

"Senior's issues – prepare yourself well in advance – make choices about how and where you want to live when you get too old to look after yourself . . .

"Dying with dignity. Make choices about how you want to die before it is too late . . .

"I saw my own mother go into a facility and die there. I never thought it would happen that way . . .

"I have a representative agreement and a will. If I am unable to look after my own money or health issues, I have legal paperwork in place so that my wishes will be fulfilled, and I have friends that will help me. One of the important things for me is to stay at home – not to go into a facility . . .

"These are just a few of the many issues facing self advocates today . . ."

10) Do you have plans to write any more books after this one?

"Oh, I might write a new Harry Potter, but mine will be called MARY Potter. The idea is that the sky is the limit – don't let people tell you that you can't do it . . .

"Perhaps a workbook for people with diversibilities on how to become a self advocate . . .

"Or a book of quotes and poetry. Maybe a recipe book called Goode Food – Goode Friends . . ."

People had lots of goode questions for us, and the presentation went very well. Parts of it were quite emotional for people, but I felt like it was important to be honest about the process of writing an autobiography, and the truth is that some parts of this process are difficult.

After the presentation, debriefing
with Zev and some gelato!

Last Thoughts

What Went Wrong?

This is the story of four people:
Everybody, Somebody, Anybody and Nobody

There was an important job to be done, and
Everybody was sure that Somebody would do it.

Anybody could have done it,
But Nobody did it.

Somebody got angry because
It was Everybody's job.

Everybody thought that
Somebody would do it.

But Nobody
Asked Anybody

It ended up that the job wasn't done, and
Everybody blamed Somebody, when actually
Nobody asked Anybody

Author unknown

Awards

I am proud of my awards, and all my awards are important to me, but I honestly feel like it takes a whole bunch of people to work towards something meaningful, so in my mind everyone who ever worked with me, or encouraged me, shares my awards.

In different ways over the years, whenever I accept awards I always say that I do what I do along with other people. I feel that other people are always a part of my awards; people who are involved with me or who are there for me when I need them.

Me with my Mom and Dad after I won the VanDusen Community Service Award in 2006.

When I accept awards, I sometimes I like to be goofy and pretend I'm at the Oscars. I'll say, "I want to thank..." and then I list off my co-workers and my parents and some of my close friends.

So, like I said, I feel very happy and proud to get an award, but at the same time I can't help sometimes feeling bad for the other people who worked so hard along with me.

The reason I do what I do is that I like the work – it's important and it's rewarding. And I have met so many incredible people.

I thought that maybe a goode way to show some of my awards without seeming like I have too a big of a head would be to take a photo of a selection of awards – some of the ones that mean the most to me.

Shown (from left to right and back to front) are my Canada Volunteer Award (1987), my Queen's Golden Jubilee Award (2002), my W.J. VanDusen Community Service Award (2006), my People First Rosemary Dybwad Award (1993), my CLBC Lifetime Achievement Award, my CLBC WOW Award (2010), my Inclusion International Lifetime Achievement Award (2008), and my B.C. Coalition of People with Disabilities Millennium Award (2000).

There are three clear glass awards that you can barely see in the photo. Two (my CLBC awards) are in the middle of the table and one (my B.C. Coalition for People with Disabilities Award) is on the front right hand side.

Glossary

Affirm- to declare that something is true

Affirmation- positive self-talk

Agenda- a list of items to be discussed

Amanuensis – a secretary or scribe who assists someone to write down their story

Articulate – able to express oneself clearly

Compassion- being sympathetic and understanding

Concur- to agree or to see eye to eye with someone

Consensus- general or widespread agreement

Context- the background information that helps to explain meaning

Diversibility- used instead of disability, because it puts the focus on a person's gifts and achievements

Empower- to give a person power and authority

Encourage- to give confidence

Establish- to set up

Forfeit- to part with, to give up something

Formidable- challenging to deal with

Hierarchy- a group arranged by rank

Humble- modest and unassuming

Impact- a powerful effect

Incompetence- lacking the skill to do something properly

Insidious- slowly harmful or destructive

Integration- becoming an accepted member of the community

Internment- imprisonment

Itinerary- travel schedule

Lenient- tolerant, not strict

Literacy- knowledge of reading and writing

Moratorium- a period of postponement, to put something off in order to think it through

Non-therapeutic- not for the treatment or prevention of disease

Oppression- harsh or cruel power over someone

Parallel- at the same time

Phenomenon- a fact that can be observed

Pioneering- a person or group who comes up with something new or original

Prejudice- a pre-formed, unfavourable opinion

Progressive- someone who advocates for social reforms

Quirk- an odd mannerism of someone's character

Scrutinize- to examine carefully

Segregate- keeping students apart based on their disabilities

Self-effacing- tending to be modest and joking at one's own expense

Sentimental- experiencing tender, romantic, or nostalgic feelings

Stereotype- to reduce someone to an oversimplified image of an entire group of people

Subsidize- to reduce the cost of something by having some of the funds provided through a public source

Transcript- a written record

Tubal litigation- a surgical method to permanently stop women from having babies

Vaguely- not clearly felt, understood, or recalled

Some Friends

Karla Verschoor

Barb and I decided to take a road trip to Whistler to check out the hotel for an upcoming conference. Barb called it my birthday trip, because I was out of town for my birthday and we did not get a chance to celebrate together.

The hotel was nice and we had a delicious lunch, but we both just wanted to get our toes wet. We followed a truck with a load of boats in the hope of finding a lake. Unfortunately, we ended up at the tour company's parking lot! We finally made our way to Lost Lake only to find "no parking" signs everywhere.

Not giving up, we decided to leave Whistler for a familiar spot. We decided to stop at Alice Lake on our way back to Vancouver.

Once we arrived, we both instantly took off our shoes and made our way to the water. It was perfect! The sun was hot, the water was cool and I looked over at Barb and we both started laughing straight from the belly.

I started to get cold and made my way to the shore, but Barb stayed in the water. There was a little girl who really wanted to share the secret of a great sandcastle. To my surprise the secret was simply wet sand. This also made me laugh a little. After taking a few buckets from the water line up to her brother who was clearly the engineer on the project, she stopped to talk to me again. She looked me straight in the eye and said with such conviction, "I am allowed to go in the water because I am wearing my bathing suit." I looked over at Barb and she gave a small curtsey. Barb and I started to laugh and the little girl went back to her building. I don't think it was the little girl's innocent ways, or the contrast of water and sun, or the sheer sense of freedom of the day that makes this memory stand out for me. It was Barb. A friend I knew was in the exact place and exact time, feeling the exact same way.

Aaron Johannes

The thing about my relationship with Barb is that she constantly challenges my assumptions about everything! I really have to keep thinking hard to keep up. It's been like this from the very beginning.

I had been involved with B.C. People First as a provincial advisor for about fourteen years and had heard so much about Barb from my friends on the board there - she was a bit of a goddess to them all. She made people feel safe and capable. However, I never actually met her as she was involved in other things by then, and then about four years ago we finally met. She was wonderful, but crowded with people who wanted her attention; she was very gracious.

A month later I was at the mall food fair with my son, who was seven, trying to decide what to eat. I looked over and there was Barb, but I assumed she wouldn't remember me so didn't say anything to her.

So this is our family story about Barb, which has become an important part of our family mythology. My son said, "I don't really want dinner, Pop, I just want ice cream." I said, "Just look around, do you see anyone else just eating ice cream for dinner?" "No," he said. "Well, there you go," I said, "people don't have ice cream for dinner – they have dinner and then they have ice cream for dessert." "Okay," he said and we went off to get some noodles for dinner, which he sort of picked at, just waiting until he could have ice cream.

Finally, I said, "Okay, let's go get some ice cream." He's always been really, really skinny and it's important just to get some food into him. We went to the ice cream place and there was Barb in the line-up.

"You probably don't remember me," I said. "Of course I do," she said. I introduced her to my son, and he was tiny and cute and people often treat him like something sort of precious, but she just talked to him like an equal. He told her that we'd had our dinner and now were going to have ice cream.

"And what did you have for dinner?" he asked her.

"This is my dinner," she said, "– I'm having ice cream."

My son turned to me with this horrified expression, looking totally shocked. It was probably the first moment (that we all have) when he realized that parents might not be the complete authority all the time (and if you're going to learn this, who better to learn it from than Barb?). It was pretty funny.

"Pop says that you need to have dinner *before* you have dessert!"

Barb nodded, and said something like, "Well that's what my parents said to me too, when I was little, but now I'm an adult and I think every once in a while you should just do something like have ice cream for dinner, have some fun instead of doing what you're supposed to do."

Aaron, Zev and I at the 2010 Celebration of Stories in Community Living hosted by Spectrum Society, 101friends.ca and Vela Microboard Association. We are standing in front of a big drawing of "hospitality" – in what they called the "Barb Goode Welcomes You" room – where the snacks and tea and hugs were!

So now our tradition, every couple of months, is an ice cream dinner. It's one of our favourite things and something that I think he'll never forget about, years from now. A seizing of joy, a rupture in the rules. And he'll never forget meeting Barb, who he used to refer to as "the ice cream lady" but now says, "our friend, Barb."

Barb's way with children is another

of those things that we could all take a lesson from, I think. She takes them so seriously, she doesn't talk down to them, and she listens to them so carefully. One of our friends was talking about how their child, who didn't really warm up to anyone, instantly felt right at home with her and was sharing secrets that she hadn't told anyone else. I think Barb's ability to speak from her heart resonates for children.

Shelley Nessman

Barb and I were presenting together at a conference a wonderful day filled with laughter, learning, and we were energized!   After our session our goode friend Karla proposed that we relax together before dinner in the lounge. It was a beautiful early summer day and we happy to find that we could sit out on the patio, which was filled with people we knew and that Barb had a long history with.   Fred Ford, James White and host of people around Barb – she was a happy camper!

Karla and I decided we would make it a martini visit . . . ☺ Barb sat quietly and I could tell that something was brewing in that head of hers . . .

Along came the waitress and asked Barb what she would like. Barb had been taking her time thinking about her order and she said, "I'll have a virgin tequila sunrise, please."   Karla and I who are known to tease Barb mercilessly both chimed in, "Uh, Barb, that is a glass of orange juice you are ordering – get the tequila – come on Barb, live a little!"

So Barb in her infinite wisdom and with a look of mischief on her face said to the waitress – "O.K. I'll have it on the side." We sat in the sunshine, enjoying snacks and reminiscing about old times and of course sipping our drinks.

When her orange juice with tequila on the side arrived – Barb cautiously dripped some of the tequila into her glass and toasted us all and took a sip.

A few minutes later Barb who was sitting next to me tugged on my sweater sleeve, a look of grave concern on her face... "What, Barb?" I asked. (She looked seriously worried about something.)

"Shelley," she said, "I think something is wrong with the tequila!"

I asked her why she thought that and she looked at me and said very loudly, "MY LIPS ARE NUMB!"

Hilarity broke out on the patio and all of Barb's seasoned drinking friends assured her there was nothing wrong with the tequila, in fact the tequila was doing exactly what it was supposed to do and that numb lips were considered a pleasant by-product of drinking it.

The best part of this story is that Barb decided that she would prefer to feel her lips for the rest of the night and timidly asked me if I would like to finish the tequila. I helped her out as a goode friend by accepting her offer and enjoying a bonus shot – pass the lime please...

Barb and I had known each other for 30-odd years, but something changed that day – our friendship grew and deepened. I think it has something to do with taking a risk with a friend and trusting a person. I also think it has something to do with sharing tequila!

Note on the photographs and quotations used in this book

Many of the photos, quotations and clippings that illustrate this book are from the Goode family collection. As these were for personal reasons, their sources, photographers or those in the photos might not be known to us. Attributions have been made wherever possible but if you know of something that should be credited, please let us know so we can correct future versions.

Afterword

By Aaron Johannes, Director,
Research, Training and Development, Spectrum Society and
Publisher, Spectrum Press

Spectrum Press is part of our agency, Spectrum Society, which has supported people with disabilities in their neighbourhoods for more than 25 years now. All around you will find our motto, *"Express yourself. Build your network. Find your voice."* These ideas of what's important in people's lives were given to us by those we support, their families, friends and neighbours. Spectrum Press hopes to be part of this idea of self-expression, listening, network building through supporting either people who honour these voices, or through the facilitation of voices that have not been heard from enough.

As of this year we will publish our sixth book or DVD, all of which we hope will further the cause of self-determination in the world, beginning with our own province. In our workshops, classes and facilitated groups, we have spoken to more than 3000 people in places ranging from Nashville to the far North. In all of these efforts we are proud that people with disabilities (or, "diversibilities"), such as Barb, are our colleagues and co-workers.

Barb is an example of someone who does express herself, who supports the self-expression of others, insisting (in her gentle but firm way) on language everyone can understand, who has developed and tended her own network which she freely shares. She's found her voice.

There could be no better choice for our first publication by a self advocate. We feel honoured that she entrusted us with a role in this important goal of hers, as we work to achieve our own vison to create materials that will lead to further leadership, individualized services and autonomy for people with disabilities and their networks.

One of the things we liked about this book is that it's a different voice, of a personality aware of autonomy and diversity more than most. The idea that part of one's biography is the recipes that have been handed down – the importance of food and memories and meetings that we share – that there are moments when the right quote, or the right poem, or a photograph of Hawaii that your parents took for you ("take a moment"), or a shared story with a friend – and that, in fact, our friends write part of our stories – all these things keep all of us strong and capable or... "diversible."

From the beginning, this mix of experiences has been Barb's vision of her story. Barb's dad, Norm, said, "You don't show people you can do something by talking about it; you show them you can do it by doing it." However, writing your own story, in a world where few people like yourself have told such stories, is hard. We watched her wrestle through some tough moments, exult in some wonderful memories, remember and claim some successes and, at the same time, we watched her get engaged to be married and begin to move on into yet another chapter of her life. I notice she didn't end this with "The End."

Really, this is a love story. The love of some amazing parents who quietly charted new territory for their daughter, and saw what they did as simply what needed doing, to make the world right, and then, perhaps even harder for parents, stood solidly beside her while she charted her own journeys all around the globe. When Barb writes about not wanting her parents to know she was lost in an airport, waiting for hours, one can sense that her parents already knew, that they were taking deep breaths and being okay with their daughter's mission of service. We've been considering sending our son on a plane by himself for the first time – a one hour trip, no plane changes, no stopovers – it's so hard. Imagine the Goode family at home while Barb was travelling through India, New Zealand, Africa, Hungary, and who knows where else, spreading her message of hope and pride. Unimaginable love.

It is also the story of Barb and Harold, two of the most respected members of one of the final and most complex civil rights movements – you see them together in photograph after photograph as they move from cause to cause, decade to decade. What might they accomplish together once they get married?

And so much love from those who have supported Barb over the years, who have been called to her mission of equality and fairness for everyone.

And, from Barb, this boundless love for all those she has met who she wants us to hear the voices of . . . It's hard not to wonder about the tally of lives she's touched around the world. As Al says that she is *"one of the foremost builders of the modern day disability movement. A hero who deserves to be included in the same breath as Terry Fox and*

Rick Hansen." Heroic indeed, but also simply a "goode" friend to so many.

Someone asked me once what my real agenda in my chosen field is and I said, "I'd like people with disabilities to be in elected office." They thought I was joking, but I wasn't. I would trust folks like Harold and Barb more than most... and imagine how they might get communities participating in democracy? Interestingly, when we announced the publication of Barb's book, a self-advocate wrote and said, "If she wanted to be Prime Minister, I would vote for her." Me too.

The other part of this story is, of course, Jim. There is an old word, Amanuensis, (it's okay, Barb, I took the liberty of adding it to your glossary) which means someone who is like a secretary, or a scribe, who would write down the words spoken by the person who hired them or, sometimes, by the prophets. Sometimes you find the word in poems, where it can mean someone who writes down what is inspired by the gods, or someone who inspires. In our agency Jim has had many roles and in this most recent one has been so clearly inspired and felt honoured to spend time with Barb.

Wolf Wolfensberger, in a lovely article titled, "What Advocates Have Said," which is about how ordinary people's lives have been enriched by intentional relationships with people with disabilities, wrote, "However, something also tends to get lost as compared to the advocate's own words--perhaps unpolished, poorly organized, and laconic, and yet with such a ring of truth, and so compelling. Many of the things that they say are apt to be edited out if someone else wrote their story." This is true of all of our stories, but particularly those who are so used to having what they say interpreted to fit into another's agenda.

Several times in the writing Jim has told us things on the order of, "I am being transformed." He's been a role model for many in helping her tell this story – not more than she ever asked for, and listening so carefully to make sure he was really hearing what she wanted and needed, without assumptions. We've always had huge respect for Jim – one of the best people we've known in our quarter century of service – but this writing project has shown him at his peak and, as with the choice of Barb as our first self advocate author, being able to work with Jim as our first Amaneunsis has also been a gift.

February 2011

Jim Reynolds, Manager,
Social Enterprises,
Spectrum Society for
Community Living

Jim has worked in social services for more than 25 years. He started out working in an outreach service for seniors living in Vancouver's downtown east-side, and has been a manager for Spectrum Society since 1990. Jim lives in Vancouver with his partner and their two cats.

His passions are writing, reading and jazz music. He hosts a book collecting website at www.jamespreynolds.com and has written three novels. He is a co-author of *101 Ways To Facilitate Making Friends: Ideas and conversation starters for people with disabilities and their supporters – A FACILITATION MANUAL,* along with Aaron Johannes and Susan Stanfield.

Spectrum Press
A DIVISION OF SPECTRUM SOCIETY FOR COMMUNITY LIVING

Spectrum Press publishes approximately
five books and/or DVDs each year
by, with or about self-advocates, self-determination,
support networks and best-practices

The 101 Friends Project
conducts community based research projects
facilitates and hosts workshops
and encourages person-centred best practices
and partnership

To learn more about our work
visit www.101friends.ca
or www.spectrumsociety.org